T0294121

'David Sharpe was a great talent and
is a genuine character. His fascinating
memoir is honest about the roller-coaster of
world-class athletics.'

Colin Youngson,
distance-running historian

'A brutally honest exposé of David's life on and
off the track. I couldn't put it down.'

Greg Whitfield, 800m Running Page
Facebook group founder

'Wow! What a brilliant read. Insightful,
searingly honest, very funny and so moving at
times, I really felt that I was there with David.'

Diane Hedley, daughter of the late
Jimmy Hedley OBE, David's coach

DAVID
SHARPE
ENIGMA ON TRACK

Foreword by
Steve Cram

DAVID
SHARPE
ENIGMA ON TRACK

Wild Child
to World Champion

David Sharpe
and Brian Gardner

First published by Pitch Publishing, 2023

Pitch Publishing
9 Donnington Park,
85 Birdham Road,
Chichester,
West Sussex,
PO20 7AJ
www.pitchpublishing.co.uk
info@pitchpublishing.co.uk

© 2023, David Sharpe, with Brian Gardner

ISBN 978 1 80150 679 3

Typesetting and origination by Pitch Publishing
Printed and bound in Great Britain by TJ Books, Padstow

Contents

Contents

For Jimmy

Foreword by Steve Cram

TO DESCRIBE any individual as a mercurial talent conjures up a myriad of images, especially in sport. However, in the case of David Sharpe, or 'Sharpey' to all who know him, it could not be more apt. From the moment he turned up at our track in Jarrow with his shock of red hair and toothy grin he had everyone's attention. Initially it was his raw running ability that raised eyebrows but increasingly we got to know the character that would set Sharpey apart from the rest.

It would be easy to summarise Sharpey's journey to the top of the world in athletics as unconventional or even at times unbelievable, but that would genuinely fail to fully describe the unique environment and approach that he has always seemed to inhabit. This book is a fulsome account of his side of the story, told in the same non-compromising style that epitomises his outlook on life. No frills or embellishment; just an

11

honest, entertaining and engrossing insight into his world and all of its facets.

The young man from Jarrow who was thrust on to the world stage seemed to decide that in order to survive and prosper in an unfamiliar environment it was best to stay exactly as he was. Thank goodness he did. Time and again he has chosen the path that suits him, on and off the track, not without incident or consequence. Sometimes the results were awesome; at other times less so but all met with the same unflinching honesty and integrity.

To this day I am still telling anecdotes about Sharpey to those in the athletics world who know little of him, but they always produce a laugh at his antics or a nod of respect for his achievements. As this book recounts, he is so much more than a former athlete. It is his charging down the home straight from the back of the field or his cheeky laugh to cover a misdemeanour or faux pas that I will always treasure.

I am sure that *David Sharpe: Enigma on Track* will give as much enjoyment to the reader as Sharpey has given to all of us lucky enough to be part of his journey.

Steve Cram CBE, former world champion at 1500 metres and world record holder at 1500 metres, 2000 metres and the mile

Introduction

DAVID SHARPE was an enigmatic international athlete during the 80s and 90s. He was known for his trademark late finishes and erratic lifestyle. He describes his background in Jarrow as 'humble', from which he rose to become World Junior and European Indoor champion and World Cup winner – all at 800 metres. His best time of 1:43.98 was number one in the UK in 1992. He trained with Steve Cram and was coached by the legendary Jimmy Hedley.

David is still a popular figure in his native North East, and has a fascinating and often amusing story to tell. However, it's not all race reports and funny stories. David provides insight into not only his training and relationship with Jimmy, but also a wide range of activities such as motorbiking, skiing, celebrity boxing, travelling overseas, birdwatching and getting into trouble with authority. He also reflects eloquently upon suspected drug use, athlete payments, cancer, bereavement and suicide. He speaks with pride about his family, friends and achievements, and with regret about controversial and sometimes shocking incidents. David's story is as entertaining as his running once was.

On your marks ... for a rollicking read!

* * *

Brian Gardner is the author of *No Cross-Country for Old Men* and *As Others See Us*. A graduate in English literature and former masters international athlete, he was a primary school teacher, fitness instructor, and manager/team leader in physical activity and public health.

Prologue

Jimmy's Magic Wand

Athens, Greece, 1986

'RIGHT, ME bonny lad,' said Jimmy. 'I've watched your heat and I've watched your semi, and I've watched all the rest, and I'm telling you now, there's nobody can touch you. Your turn of speed, and how you've run. Nobody's going to beat you today.'

I was fortunate to have my coach, Jimmy Hedley, with me at the World Junior Championships. Jimmy would look at a runner and comment on their physique, their style and how they flowed, how they stood out from the rest. Jimmy was a natural, rather than getting all technical. He knew what he was doing, alright.

I'll never forget what Jimmy said before the final of the 800 metres. He was the type of person – if he didn't know or think something – he wouldn't say it. (There were lots of times when he *didn't* say what he did before a race.) And I was thinking, *Bliddy hell, that gives me a lot of confidence.*

While Jimmy was speaking, I was bending over and he was pouring cold water over the back of my head, so it didn't run down my front and soak my vest and number. Ginger-haired, I had a problem with the heat in Athens. I'd stay in the shade and make sure I had plenty of water on me.

Now it was five minutes before we were called to the start line, and Jimmy was telling me I was going to win.

And, do you know, Jimmy was right.

* * *

Jimmy had wangled it so that we arrived in Athens a week before the rest of the team. The hotelier said that we couldn't stay in the team hotel because there were no reservations in our names. But Jimmy had sorted it for us, although we didn't even know who was paying for it.

For some reason, we couldn't get on the track to train. All my sessions of 10 x 150 metres or 5 x 200 metres at a really fast pace were done in the local park in the middle of the city. No spikes, just in trainers, and that's the way it was. Had I been a lot more serious I'd have tried to persuade someone to let us into the stadium to do proper track work with proper spikes and proper times.

But all Jimmy said was, 'Right, if we cannot get on to the track we'll go down to the park and you'll do your reps there.' And that's how it worked.

And then there was Jimmy and his cats. He loved cats. When we got to the park to train, he said to me, 'Where's all these cats coming from? Look at the state of them, there's nowt on them.'

That's when we found out that they were all feral. So Jimmy started taking chicken off our plates, wrapping it up in a hanky and putting it in his pockets to feed all the wild cats in Athens. There was me doing my reps in the park, and Jimmy surrounded by about 20 feral cats, all jumping up for their chicken.

* * *

On the start line, looking along my lane, I remember thinking it was weird because the stadium seemed half-empty, although there must have been about 15,000 or 20,000 people. It's hard to describe how I felt from the gun until the finish line, what went on or what I was thinking, because in most races the only thing that's going through your mind is that you're trying to keep up with somebody who's at the front.

After the gun went, what was going on around us was just a blur. I was in the zone, and didn't really hear any noise in the background. It was silent until I hit the home straight, where the stand was full and I could hear the crowd noise build up. I can remember feeling that going through the first lap in about 54 seconds was pretty easy. For me to take it up with 300 metres to go was unusual. I must have been feeling that confident, although I didn't really know at the time how much quicker I'd run before than all the other competitors. When I hit the last 120 metres or so, the roar of the crowd was suddenly right there with me. I think I took about ten metres out of everyone. It was a race I won quite comfortably in one minute, 48.32 seconds (1:48.32).

When I finished, I took things in a bit more. World champion! I was over the moon, absolutely delighted.

Jimmy asked, 'Do you realise what you've just done? You're the best in the world.'

And I said, 'But not everybody in the world runs 800 metres, do they?'

'But do you know how many *do* run 800 metres?' Jimmy asked me. 'Think of all them you had to beat to get chosen for Great Britain. And then think about all the other countries.'

It was unique: only three years earlier we'd had the first-ever World Championships for seniors, and Crammy (Steve Cram) won the 1500 metres. So here we'd got somebody with the same coach, from the same club, winning the 800 metres at the first-ever World Championships for juniors. It can never happen again.

When Jimmy was asked how it felt to coach two of the first-ever world champions in middle distance, he said, 'Ah, well, I've got a magic wand, haven't I?'

* * *

At the end of the championships, we couldn't get the bill sorted out for the extra week that we'd stayed in the hotel. We were ready to leave and the hotelier asked us to pay for the first week.

Jimmy said, 'What do you mean? He's the world champion, he's not paying.' That wasn't Jimmy being offish, that was just Jimmy being Jimmy, which I often found hilarious.

And the hotelier said, 'You here from this date and we have payment for these dates only, and we need payment for those dates.'

And Jimmy said, 'Well, it'll be the same people who are paying for the rest of the team, it'll be the British Athletics.'

'Hold on a minute, Jimmy,' I said, 'I'll ring John Hockey [my agent].' This was typical of how me and Jimmy worked together.

I assume that John rang Andy Norman (the athletics promoter) and got the hotel bill paid, because, when I got back home, Andy said, 'Sharpey, it's a good job you fucken won that race, because you'd have been paying your own fucken hotel bill if you hadn't won.'

He probably wouldn't have made us pay, but that was Andy down to a T.

It was a good trip, and a good season. My fastest time was 1:45.64 that year, which I think was two or three seconds faster than any other UK junior. I never knew what was coming next, but Jimmy did. He knew that there were bigger things to come.

* * *

Back home in Jarrow, our core training group was eight to ten local athletes. Sometimes we had people training with us from all over the country, and it wasn't long after the World Juniors that somebody came over from New Zealand to join our group. People could just waltz up and watch the type of reps that me and Crammy did, or train with us and our coach.

But, for me, life carried on as normal. Having a great interest in other things, I had motorbikes, wildlife and all that in the back of my mind. I was especially fascinated by golden eagles. And remember, this was all happening when I was 18 and 19.

I had a great relationship with Jimmy – a fantastic motivator, coach and friend – but it was very difficult for him to get me to change my ways. I'd train my bollocks off on the track, but I couldn't stand getting up on a Sunday morning and going out to run ten miles. My training was that high intensity, it was enough to get me by. But to have run the times I ran, and achieve what I achieved on only about 25 miles a week at times, it's embarrassing trying to explain to people how much of it was natural talent.

And I was a lazy so-and-so. Had I not won at the World Juniors, I'd have been disappointed but I wouldn't have been down in the dumps or devastated. If I didn't run well, the disappointment didn't last long, maybe a day or two. If I'd had more drive, and if running not so well as I should have done had given me a kick up the backside and spurred me on to train harder, I might have gone to the Olympics and done really well. But I was a happy-go-lucky type of person with this blasé attitude that didn't let anything bother me.

If I'd finished third or fourth, I'd have said, 'It's not bad for somebody whose golden ambitions aren't always about athletics.'

There's much more to me than just running.

Chapter One

Wild Child

Jarrow, England, the 70s

I REMEMBER my first day at nursery like it was yesterday. My dad was getting me ready and saying, 'Don't worry, it's only for a few hours, I'll be back at two o'clock to pick ye up.'

And that set something off in my brain for me to go apeshit. My dad had to carry me there, which was only about 400 metres from where we lived, and I was wriggling and crying and screaming all the way. My temper was sometimes off the Richter scale. Going through the gates of the nursery, as soon as he put me down that was it, I was away like a shot. And if it hadn't been for a woman who stopped me at the gate, I'd have been back home in no time. She picked me up, her hands underneath my arms, and passed me back to my dad.

Looking back now, I don't know how fast I ran but that was the beginning of me having this extra energy and burst of speed. I can't remember anything else about nursery. But that particular day sticks in my head.

I was a wild child from Jarrow. There were things I did as a kid that I don't think were normal. I used to always be reminded by my mam and nanna of something that I did when I was five or six, although I can't honestly remember doing it. They were trying to get me in from playing in the garden, to get ready for my bed, but I didn't want to. And I always had to get my own way, which was a nightmare for my mam and nanna. If my dad had been home, it wouldn't have been a problem. He was a sort of disciplinarian, and if I was clarting about in the back garden, up to no good, and he wanted me in, I'd come in. But he'd work backshifts and nightshifts, and on this occasion he wasn't home. So I was giving my mam and nanna a hard time.

Anyway, eventually they made me come in. And with my fierce temper, being exceptionally hyper and at times uncontrollable, I had to get back at them. What was the worst thing I could possibly do?

It was a Sunday, when my mam always washed our whites. So I went and found a lump of coal from the back garden, and because they'd made me come in early, it went in the washer. It's something I can't remember doing, but up until about 30 years later, I was often reminded of it. The washer was supposed to wash your whites whiter than white, but not on that black Sunday. For me, it was payback.

I was always climbing everywhere. I had a problem sleeping (still do). When I was about eight years old, I'd go to bed and wait for my parents to go to theirs. Then I'd get up and climb down the banister to the bottom of the stairs. I'd have to touch the floor to go into the sitting room, but then I'd go round the sitting room from one chair to the three-piece to another chair, into the kitchen, over all the kitchen units, back the way I came, all without stepping on the floor, then I'd have to touch down just once again to get back up the stairs. It was a challenge, and I'd have done the whole thing off the floor if it hadn't been for that one step to get into the sitting room. Now, I don't know whether that's normal or not. I don't suppose it is.

If it wasn't climbing, it was jumping over things. Our garden wall was four or five feet away from the grass with a path in between. I'd try to jump from the grass and over the wall without touching the path. I managed to do it but I landed on my shin and took a chunk out of it. What happened next was one of my regular visits to A&E. I had to have eight stitches, and I've still got the scar.

I loved wildlife and still do. As a child, instead of just watching birds flying about, I'd take it upon myself to try to catch them. I'd put a bit of bread in a bucket, and attach a bit of string going up from the garden to my bedroom window. I'd watch from the window, and as soon as a sparrow or a blackbird went into the bucket I'd pull on the string and trap it. Watching birds wasn't enough for me, I needed to get closer, one way or another. I wanted to handle them before I let them go.

We had a cabin in the back garden, and I noticed that the birds would feed from the top of it. So I climbed up on the cabin roof to try to catch them. I didn't know that Dad was watching me until I heard him shouting, 'What the bliddy hell d'ye think ye're doin?' This gave me a shock and I jumped off, but didn't see the washing line, which tipped me upside down and flipped me on to my back and neck with a thud. I was so winded that I couldn't breathe and I'd ripped my hand open as well. So it was another trip to A&E, and seven stitches in my hand.

There's a photo of the family at the start of our holidays, me with 15 stitches: eight in my shin and seven in the hand. And we hadn't even reached Blackpool yet. I was accident-prone alright. But nothing would stop me messing about, running, jumping or climbing, even when the police came to our door after I was seen up on the school roof.

Dad used to work in a chemical factory in Jarrow. I'm sure he wasn't supposed to do this, but he brought stuff home from work and kept an array of little bottles in his cabin. He'd tell me about the different chemicals. This one would go into lipsticks, that one into creams and another into hair dye.

As a kid I was always out where I shouldn't have been and coming home covered in oil or paint or muck. Dad would take me down to the cabin, open one of his bottles and use what was inside to wipe the muck off me. I was never sure what it was that he put on me.

Dad would shower as soon as he came in from work, and then he'd pay me 50 pence to comb his hair. That might sound weird, but no matter how much he showered, he could never get rid of this pungent smell coming off him and these tiny grains, like salt, stuck in his hair. Whatever they were (something to do with the chemicals), they gave off this smell.

One night my mam had a bad head, and Dad said he'd go to the cabin and sort it out. I had my pyjamas on and followed him, but he said, 'Get out the way, cos this is bliddy dangerous. It's for your ma's bad head.' I saw this little clear jar with a black top. Dad took the top off it and said, 'Right, Mary, I'm going to put this under your nose. Don't snort it up hard, just take a tiny, tiny sniff.'

But Mam took a big snort, and I was thinking, *We're gonna need an ambulance here.* When I smelled it, I don't know how to describe it, it was like the worst thing you could ever smell. So, what it was like for Mam with it right up her nose, I can't imagine. She had tears coming down from her eyes, she was struggling to breathe, coughing and spluttering, and she started going haywire. After a couple of minutes of this she said, 'What have ye done to me?'

And Dad, laughing, said, 'Yer bad head's gone now, hasn't it? I told ye not to bliddy sniff it!' Mam recovered eventually, but she never let Dad forget it. I didn't find out until a long time afterwards that it was ammonia, although it might have been watered down.

Dad was generally a quiet person but he had a sneaky sense of humour, which he passed on to me. One of his workmates told me a story about when he hid inside a barrel in a dark corridor at work, ready to jump out and give his pals a fright. The only problem was, when he jumped out he banged his head on some metal piping and gave himself more than a fright. I'd always wondered how he got that bruise on his head.

Years later, a link between the chemicals at the factory and cancer was found. Dad had always said that working with benzene and formaldehyde was dangerous, that he'd be lucky to live another two or three years and he wouldn't live to 50, then 60, then 70. He said it right up until a couple of weeks before he went into hospital with a stomach tumour, which killed him at the age of 81. But he'd outlived a lot of his friends who worked with him at that factory. They all died of cancer-related illnesses long before my dad. The factory's been closed for years. That kind of thing wouldn't be allowed nowadays.

Dad used to be a fast sprinter, and my brother Robert (Bob, although I always called him 'Our Lad'), who's four years older than me, was a good footballer. Lewis, Robert's son (my nephew), went on to be a soccer star for Georgia Gwinnett Grizzlies. So there must be something in the genes as well as all those chemicals.

Everywhere I went, I ran. Our Lad and I would run up to the nearest field to our house and spend hours playing football one-on-one. Jumpers for goalposts, of course. Our Lad was mad about football and better than me, so it was always me who had to go in goal first. On a weeknight we'd be there for a couple of hours and come back only when it got dark or we were hungry. But on a weekend we'd spend half a day at it.

When I was about 12, my mam would send me to the nearest chip shop, probably about 500 metres away, where the queue was out the door and I didn't want to wait. Rather than stand for ten or 15 minutes, I'd run to the next chip shop, more than a mile away. It's things like that make me think it was all about running off extra energy, usually getting out in the fresh air.

I had no idea at the time that this was probably unusual behaviour. Whether you want to call it ADHD or not, I don't know. I think it was. In those days I don't know whether ADHD was a thing. Throughout my life I was never diagnosed with anything. And now, at the age of 55, I still have trouble concentrating on one thing at a time.

In the last 30 years I've coached thousands of kids, from Reception up to Year Six. Looking back at what I did on the chip shop trip, I wonder, out of all those children, how many of them, if their mothers sent them to get chips, would just wait in the queue. I'd probably say about 99 per cent of them. Except this scatty one sitting here.

Chapter Two

A Zest for Speed

Jarrow, England, the early 80s

THE FIRST race I remember winning was at St Matthew's Primary School Sports Day. It seemed like miles at the time but it was only five laps of the football pitch. Then going onto St Joseph's, I won the 100 metres, 200 metres, 400 metres, 800 metres, long jump, triple jump and high jump, purely because of natural ability and having spent so much of my childhood jumping around in the back garden. And having a zest for speed. One thing was leading to another, but I hadn't found athletics yet. Then athletics found me.

When I was 14 and in the YMCA, I won a ten kilometres fun run, which was quite good for a young lad who didn't really run much. That's when a guy called Geordie Heslop said that I needed to join an athletics club. He said that running was something that I excelled in, and couldn't be ignored any longer.

So I joined Jarrow & Hebburn AC, my first and, as it turned out, only club. Tommy Sullivan was my first coach, already in his 70s when I joined. Sadly, it was only about six months later that he passed away. I feel a bit guilty at times because Tommy saw the worst of me. I didn't want to race on a Saturday, I wanted to go with my friends to Westgate Road in Newcastle, where all the bike shops were, and watch everyone pulling wheelies. All the time that Tommy was coaching me, he and my dad were trying to persuade me to run on a Saturday, rather than going to watch all these blokes on motorbikes.

I'd say to my dad, 'I don't wanna go and run that race at Gateshead.'

And Dad was like, 'But Tommy's been coaching ye, and he wants ye to run.'

'But, Dad, ye know where I go every Saturday.'

And so it went on. It wasn't easy for Dad or Tommy. I was a nightmare to coach, although in the end I agreed to race on Saturdays. It got to the point that how fast I was running couldn't be brushed aside, motorbikes or not. Athletics became more important than my jaunts down the Westgate Road.

I wasn't running a lot of races for the club, but I was doing well in schools' competitions. St Joseph's ran against Springfield, where Crammy used to go to school, years before my schooldays.

The year that Tommy died I won the 800 metres in the North East Championships at Gateshead Stadium. I was 15 and I'd finally put my other interests, especially motorbikes, on the back burner. It's conjecture to say what type of coach Tommy would have been if we'd had an athlete-coach relationship for two or three years. I'll never know how that would have panned out.

Jimmy was the next coach around, and he took me under his wing. He had a wealth of experience in middle-distance training. In Crammy, he already had an athlete that he'd brought up through the ranks into world-class, and he introduced me to the same type of training that Crammy was doing. Jimmy started coaching me in 1983, the same year that Crammy won the World Championships 1500 metres. There was a group of eight or nine of us. I'd join in and do the same sessions as Crammy, but not as fast.

After my first session, Jimmy asked me, 'Do you realise how fast you've just run those reps? At your age?' I said I didn't have a clue. But Jimmy did. Like magic, he could see the future.

After leaving school at 15, I went on a Youth Training Scheme (YTS). One of my placements was in a sawmill and another was welding. Jimmy said I was like Alf Tupper, but I didn't even know who the guy was. It was much later that I found out that he was a comic book character who was known as 'The Tough of the Track'. He worked as a welder, had fish and chips for his pre-race meal and beat all the toffs. It probably wasn't to do with the welding or even the running that Jimmy said that. It was more likely my diet, which was horrendous, right through my running career. I've been tested for diabetes twice. I haven't got it but I've tried to cut down on sugar a few times. Even back then I tried it, and I never even lasted a day. I was out running, suffering from a bad head, weak as a kitten.

People used to say that my hyperactivity was caused by too much sugar. I don't know about that but being hyperactive on the track wasn't always a bad thing. Within a year of joining Jimmy's training group I ran a 1500 metres in the Tyne League at Gateshead. It was 4 July 1984, four days before my 17th birthday, and I ran 3:46.3, which wasn't a kick in the backside off the world age best for a 16-year-old. (I ran 3:42.7 on the same track the following year.) Also around that time, I took part in my first race overseas, in Byrkjelo, Norway. I ran 800 metres in 1:51.02, which was close to the world age best held by one Peter Elliott.

It's no secret that I was lazy, but I loved track work. Our training was simple; we'd do a lot of repetition sessions. I learned this from Jimmy and Crammy, and that might have come through Brendan Foster, I don't know. I'd run 10 x 400 metres in 60 seconds with a minute's rest. (Crammy would do them in 57.) I wasn't aware at the time of lactate threshold or whatever you want to call it, but to get through ten of those you were running at your maximum.

When we ran 10 x 300 metres, which I loved, I always struggled to get back in 45 seconds from the finish line to the start of the next 300 metres. It was quite a fast jog when you were tired. That was a killer. Sometimes we'd do 10 x 200 metres with 30 seconds of recovery: a quick jog straight across the infield back to the start. I did some of those in 25 or 26 seconds. It was instilled into me that you were running almost flat out but knowing that you had ten of them to do.

There was a session I did to find out what I was capable of over 800 metres. It was 400 metres at 80 per cent intensity, five minutes rest, then another 400 metres flat out. By adding the two times together you had an idea what sort of shape you were in. You had to imagine, though, that in a race there would be no recovery. Then two or three days before the race we'd run 10 x 150 metres flat out.

What Jimmy would say is, 'You only get out of it what you put into it.' He'd say this to athletes of all standards. 'If you can get out there and work hard, do your ten miles on a Sunday morning and seven miles on a Monday and then ten 400s, not at Crammy or Sharpey's pace, but at your pace, you *will* get better and you *will* see results.'

Jimmy's training philosophy was: 'Just put the hard work in. Nowt difficult, nowt scientific. What I'm going to tell you, I've never read in a book. It's just you putting hard work in and seeing results.' And it worked for nearly all his athletes. All the ones that trained hard.

Jimmy wasn't a great believer in weights. We didn't touch them. We didn't run on sand dunes either. Steve Ovett would train on them though. Harry Wilson (his coach) and Jimmy got on well. What worked for Ovett might not have worked for Sebastian Coe or Steve Cram. We did the odd hill session but that was just to break up the monotony of what we were doing on the track, which was all hard repetitions at race pace.

We used to do a park session (which I hated, by the way) on a Saturday morning, when I'd struggled to get out of bed. Run a mile, then jog 1,000 metres from one park into another and run 2 x 1,000 metres with another 1,000 metres jog in between. Then 6 x 400 metres (which was actually a little bit longer than 400) with 400 metres jog recovery, 6 x 200 metres with 200 metres jog, and finally 6 x 150 metres flat out. The whole thing would take about an hour, and it was an absolute killer. But the thing that put me off the most was that it was at 10 o'clock on a Saturday morning, when I'd rather have been asleep.

In the winter we'd run more miles. 'Get as many miles in the tank as you can,' Jimmy would say. 'You cannot run a car on an empty tank.'

I probably failed on that because I didn't like getting out of bed for the ten-milers on a Sunday morning, as I may already have mentioned once or twice. I remember on the odd occasion reaching about 60 miles per week, but more often than not I was on only about 40, or maybe 50. I should have been doing more. I ran once a day but Crammy and others in our training group trained twice every day and sometimes ran up to 90 miles per week. To be fair to me, I suffered a lot with shin splints, and the more mileage I did, the more I suffered. So I'd often say that I was going to run five or seven miles and miss that ten-mile run on a Sunday morning. Which suited me.

From the early days and throughout my athletics career, I could never run distance in the mornings. In road or cross-country races I'd often get a stitch after two or three miles. Had they been later in the afternoon it might have been different. I could knock out five-minute miles for six miles on evening training runs no problem, but if I tried to do that on a morning or early afternoon, I was nowhere near.

My best-ever 10K was set in 1986. It was 30:17 in South Shields, and I was second to Crammy. I knew the course inside out. I got to three miles in 15 minutes and thought, *Here we go, I'm going to have a stitch and get too tired as usual.* But it didn't happen and I finished quite strongly. That was a one-off.

I didn't have any problems running quick 800 metres in championship heats early in the day, but I couldn't cope with longer distances, even at six- or seven-minute-miling pace, at the same time of day. Week in, week out, I'd get that heavy feeling in my legs.

I once (only once) ran a half-marathon in about an hour and a half, and struggled all the way round, even though I could run much faster on a nighttime in training. All these older runners were coming past me. It was driving me up the wall. When I crossed the finish line I swore that I'd never ever run one of them again. And I didn't.

Some of my best races were on the 200 metres indoor track at RAF Cosford. I'd find myself training for them, doing 10 x 200 metres or 300 metres in the middle of winter, which I enjoyed more than the ten-milers. My mileage was broken up more than most. That's another reason that it was lower than others in the group.

Back outdoors, I was in Antrim for the UK (senior) Championships in 1985. I knew there had been troubles in Northern Ireland but I didn't have a great interest in the history. That was to come later. I finished second to Tom McKean, even though I was only 16 or 17. I was to race Tom at least three times per year, year in, year out. That was the first of them.

At the end of 1985, *Athletics Weekly* magazine interviewed me and Jimmy. I actually can't remember anything about it but someone posted it on a running forum the other day. Apparently I said that I was better at 1500 metres than 800 metres. In hindsight, I was maybe repeating what other people might have thought. I've never thought that 1500 metres was my best event. It might have been or should have been 1500 metres, if that makes sense. My times over 1500 metres as a young junior were better than my 800 metres times. Crammy always said that I'd have been a better 1500 metres runner had I not been so lazy. Those two races in 3:46 and 3:42 would point towards me being a better 1500 metres runner than 800 metres. But I didn't run any faster at 1500 metres for the rest of my life, because I didn't like them one little bit. I absolutely detested 1500 metres. As far as I was concerned 1500 metres was one and three-quarter laps too far. I just wanted to be an 800 metres runner because I hated 1500 metres.

Alongside the interview there's a picture of me in a cross-country race, and the caption says, 'David is as much at home on the road and country as he is on the track.' Which I think is quite funny.

I wasn't riding motorbikes any more but in athletics I'd found another outlet for my zest for speed. Jimmy was helping me to fill up the tank, ready for the next lap. Now I come to think about it, that's quite funny because Jimmy had this ridiculous three-wheeler car, so it would only ever be at three-quarters capacity. Which is what some people said about my training. Well, we'd see about that.

Chapter Three

Surely Sharpe Will Never
Reduce that Gap

UK and overseas, 1986

JIMMY TOOK me to five races indoors early in 1986, which was going to be a big year for me. I ran against Tony Morrell in the Amateur Athletics Association (AAA) (senior) Championships. I remember more about that race than the World Juniors later the same year. Tony must have thought that there was only one way that he could beat me, and that was by going off really, really quick to try to take the sting out of me. I remember thinking, *I canna keep up with this pace*. It was way, way too fast. I was that far back with one lap to go, I was out of the TV picture.

The commentator said, 'There's a very big gap between Morrell and Sharpe, who moves into third place, but surely he will never reduce that gap.'

But although Tony was a canny athlete, he'd gone off too quickly. I came past him with only about 20 metres to go and won in 1:49.48. I didn't really pick it up a lot; I ran even pace; my splits were both 54. But because Tony had started so fast, his second half was much slower than his first. My time was a new UK junior record. The funny thing was, Mal Edwards, who was also in the race, was the one who set the record 17 years before.

As soon as the race finished, the commentator said, 'It was a race that Sharpe never seemed able to win.' (But I did win.) Later he said to me privately, 'I'm getting sick of you, Sharpey. You're making me look a fool.' He said that I was an enigma. You hadn't a clue how I was going to run. Sometimes I didn't even know myself what I was going to do, but I think people enjoyed that about my races. My tactics didn't always work, mind.

After the AAAs I was selected to run the 1000 metres for England vs USA. Through my own stupidity, I had very little sleep. The night before any race, whether it was local or international, I'd never think of drinking alcohol. Not in a million years, because it's stupid. Normally, if anyone had asked me to go out for a drink I'd have told them to go and sling their hook, but on this occasion I was persuaded by my best mate, Michael (Whitey), to go to a club in South

Shields. I was never much of a drinker, didn't like beer, lager or spirits. (Later I found that Malibu suited me though. And the odd lager top.)

I said, 'First of all, I'm not going to drink because I'm going to Cosford tomorrow to run for England and I'm getting picked up at seven o'clock in the morning.'

However, there was this new Mexican beer with a bit of lemon or lime stuck in the neck of the bottle. So we were in this nightclub at 10 o'clock at night and I was conscious that I was getting picked up early the next morning for the race. But I liked the taste of this new drink, so I had another one, and then another one, and then another. I vaguely remember three or four blokes standing at the bar looking at me but nothing happened. I didn't know them, I didn't see them properly, but I found out later that they saw me.

I wasn't used to drinking but I'd found something I liked and it went down so easy. It wasn't until half past two in the morning when I got outside that it hit me. All of a sudden I felt ill. So I wandered home, the worse for wear. It was the only time in my entire athletics career that I got half-pissed the night before a race.

I got picked up early the next morning and we got to Cosford about 11 o'clock. My race was at two o'clock and it was live on TV. But before that I was lying down for a couple of hours, feeling rough and thinking to myself, *How stupid am I?* Never again.

I won my race and we left about five o'clock, got home at nine o'clock, and I was back in the same club at 10 o'clock, celebrating my international win with a Mexican beer. So much for never again.

Now, those blokes who had seen me the night before were back in there with their wives and girlfriends. They were looking at me again and then one of the women came over and said, 'Can you settle an argument?'

I said, 'Aye, of course I can.'

'Right,' she said, 'is your name David Sharpe?'

'Yes.'

'Right, okay, were you in here last night?'

'Yes.'

And she went back to her friends, and I thought, *What's them's problem?*

Then she came back and said, 'Right, you've settled an argument, you were in here last night. But according to my husband and his mates you rolled out of here after two in the morning. Did you run a race today and, if you did, was it recorded?'

'I did, and it was live.'

So she waddled back to her friends and had a chat with them. And then she came back again and said, 'Right, so you staggered out of here early this morning, yet my husband's just seen you winning a race today. How could that be live on TV?'

So I told her again, 'Well, this is the deal: I left here at half two, got picked up at seven, went to Cosford, won the race, left there at five, got home at nine, I'm back here at ten. And it was all live. I've certainly been busy the last 24 hours.'

I don't know where they were from but I don't think they were local. People from South Shields or Jarrow would just have waltzed up and asked you straight to your face, but they kept sending her back and forth like some sort of go-between.

Drinking beer before a race is something I'm not proud of and it shouldn't have happened. It was a one-off.

At the end of that indoor season I held the UK junior records for 800 metres, 1000 metres and 1500 metres all at the same time. Then, moving outdoors, I ran the UK Championships at Cwmbran at the end of May. I was still a junior but I was nearly always running with the seniors. As we were lining up the commentator said, 'Sharpe's tactics, a little bit surprising to some veterans of the sport. But his ability, never in doubt. He leaves it late sometimes but yesterday in the heat, surprisingly, he got out in front. He doesn't like that, he likes to attack from the back.'

He wasn't the only one who was surprised. So was I, and I said I'd never do it again, especially as I was up against one of the best front-runners in the world.

'So what a prospect,' the commentator went on to say, really building the race up into a duel, even though Steve Crabb and other good athletes were in it, 'because here's a man who *only* likes to be out in front: the Rotherham steelworker, Peter Elliott.'

I don't remember why I did it but when the gun went I shot straight to the front, which the commentator must have loved, even if I didn't. He was having a field day with the drama.

'Sharpe said yesterday that he was surprised to be out in front and he wouldn't do it again but here he is, and he *is* doing it again, reluctantly, I'm sure.' He was right, you know.

'52.81 at the bell, in this wind. David's going really hard, pushing it down the back straight. Perhaps it's a successful change in his tactics.' It wasn't. Peter came past Steve Crabb and then, with only a few metres left, passed me. My tactics nearly worked. I'd just run a personal best (pb) of 1:47.01 on a windy day, finished second in the UK, and I was still only 18.

I improved to 1:46.81 at Crystal Palace for third in the AAAs. That got me selection for England versus USA at Gateshead, which I won in 1:45.88. Before 1986 I hadn't even beaten 1:50. Now I was under 1:46 and going to the World Juniors.

* * *

Not only was Jimmy a great motivator but he knew how to make me laugh too, which helped me to relax in the build-up to big races. Once we were at a car boot sale where trousers were on sale for £12 a pair or £20 for two pairs.

'They'll do me,' Jimmy said and, turning to the bloke, added, 'I'll have one pair, so that's a tenner, right?'

But the bloke said no, it was £20 for two pairs, but if he wanted only one pair it was £12.

'Oh no,' said Jimmy, 'I don't want two pairs, I only want one, and half of 20 is ten.'

'It doesn't work like that, Jimmy,' I tried to explain, but I knew he was only kidding to make me laugh. Once I got the giggles that was it, I couldn't stop, I was helpless.

He went on like this in Athens at the World Juniors too. We were walking to the park for training, Jimmy with his chicken in his pockets, all these stray cats following him, and he said, 'I'm going through two pairs of socks a day, I'm sweating that much.' And then he saw some locals and tourists wearing flip-flops, so he bought himself a pair at the market on the way. So there he was, his new flip-flops flapping about behind him, as well as the cats, and he said something like, 'I cannot keep these things on my feet, they're flapping all over the place.'

'But Jimmy,' I said, nearly collapsing with the giggles, 'that's why they're called flip-flops.'

Within minutes Jimmy had thrown them in the nearest bin, leaving me in hysterics. It was all part of his master plan. Train me hard, make me laugh, keep me relaxed. It wasn't quite a case of him telling me that I only had to keep on my feet to win, but one way or another he was building my confidence. What Jimmy did worked.

* * *

After I won the World Juniors, I was on *A Question of Sport*. Back then it was massive; everybody used to watch it. David Coleman was the question master, I was on Bill Beaumont's team with Tony Adams, and Emlyn Hughes was the other captain. A lot of people who might not have been that interested in athletics wouldn't have seen my races on TV, but *A Question of Sport* was on prime time TV. After I'd been on the programme, when I went out in South Tyneside more people recognised me. That was a turning point for me, becoming a name. It wasn't all good though; it led to me getting into trouble too. But more of that later.

During August I ran three races in a row at 1000 metres, a good distance for me. I think it was because Jimmy's training was for the 800 metres/1500 metres-type of runner, whereas Tom McKean, for instance, was training like a 400 metres runner sometimes. I still hated the 1500 metres though.

Also, in August, I travelled with the teams to the Commonwealth Games and the European Championships with Jimmy and Crammy, but I wasn't actually in the team. I'd run 1:45, was having one of my best seasons, but wasn't picked for the major championships (except the World Juniors). I might have got picked if Crammy and Coe hadn't doubled up in the 800 metres and 1500 metres. Jimmy in his wisdom – I don't know whether he'd contacted Andy Norman or somebody – was a great believer in experience. 'Look,' he said, 'young Sharpey hasn't been picked but wouldn't it be nice to send him along so that he can soak up the atmosphere and learn what it would be like if he was competing?'

So I found myself up in Edinburgh and on a flight to Stuttgart as well. I was getting used to going to major championships. Jimmy and his magic wand had wangled it again.

* * *

Also in 1986 I ran at an international athletics meeting in Mauritius. We didn't get paid to race but it was an all-expenses-paid trip for ten days. The reward was purely where it was. It was paradise.

I got to know Allan and Margot Wells really well there. The accommodation was right on the beach, and Allan and Margot and their baby daughter were upstairs and I was downstairs. It was only a little chalet, which is quite funny because Allan was built like a brick shithouse. And he's one of the nicest people I've ever come across.

I got to know Ben Johnson really well too. A few years ago I asked him whether he remembered that we used to have breakfast together in Mauritius. He was a down-to-earth bloke who was quite shy. When he got banned after the 1988 Olympics I was devastated for him. Everybody can draw their own conclusions about Ben. I liked him as a person.

When Zola Budd came to the UK I also got along well with her. There was one time when somebody handed me a leaflet outside the Gateshead Stadium. Some people were protesting that Zola shouldn't be here because of the apartheid in South Africa (her home country) and that she shouldn't be pretending that she was British. Well I crumpled up this leaflet, threw it away and told them to gang and eff off and take a hike, there was nowt wrang with her. I didn't know much about the politics. I don't know how much Zola understood them either.

* * *

It was getting near autumn when I was invited to run in a top 800 metres in Brussels, Belgium. I finished fifth in another pb, 1:45.64. A week later, back at

Crystal Palace, I ran 1:46.40. And that was the end of the season. Still a junior, I was now an established international athlete, always running against seniors. The following year I'd be a senior myself, but that wouldn't really be any different from the season just finished.

Or would it?

Chapter Four

Shin Splints and Hungary

Jarrow, England and Budapest,
Hungary, 1987–89

PEOPLE TAKE the mickey out of me because of how thin my ankles are. Honestly, you've got no idea. Even when I was training you'd very rarely see me with a pair of shorts on, because one day, when I used to wear them, I went into a school and some boy in Year Six said that his ankles were bigger than mine. This was quite funny but gave me a complex about wearing shorts. I don't know whether having very little calf muscle led to the major problems I had with shin splints.

There's a guy I used to work with, Chris Ridley, who runs marathons. We were in the canteen talking about calf and shin problems. I rolled up the bottom of my trousers to show him my ankles, and you could have heard a penny drop. He was staring, open-mouthed; he couldn't believe it. I rolled my trousers back down but he was looking and pointing and he said, 'Show us again, show us again. How did you get round the track with them?'

There were a couple of years when very little happened for me on the track, and it was always shin splints. One year the UK Championships came to Monkton Stadium and I couldn't run because I was injured. It was always the same injury. Never a calf, never a knee or an ankle, always shins. I'd sometimes try to train through it. Occasionally with shin splints and stress fractures you could get away with it, but only for a certain length of time.

I got sent to a London clinic where I ran on the treadmill and they put orthotics in my shoes. I don't think it was the way I was running, I think it was purely that my legs were so thin at the lower end. Although great athletes like Billy Konchellah or Paul Ereng had really thin lower legs as well.

I got X-rayed and that didn't show anything up, but a bone scan did. The surgeon, Dr Epstein, got my scan out and said, 'See that dark area there? That's an old stress fracture. And see that one there just below, that little dot? That's another old injury. And just below that one, that's quite recent because it hasn't gone dark yet. It hasn't healed properly.'

When stress fractures heal, I think it's like a build-up of calcium. Dr Epstein also gave me a steroid injection, nothing illegal or anything. The first time I got injected, honestly I nearly died because my shins were so thin and the needle was so thick. He stuck it into me underneath my shin bone, squeezed some of this white fluid in and turned the needle around. The pain!

He asked my permission to show the bone scans to some students, because he'd never come across anyone before with so many stress fractures.

My physio, Norman Anderson, was Crammy's physio too, and he was strength coach as well as physio to Jonathan Edwards, who became world record holder for the triple jump. It was hard for Norman because he didn't want to say, 'Look, you can't run.' He wanted to do the best he could to prepare me for a race. When he massaged the shins and put his finger into a little lump, I'd hit the roof with the pain.

I had ultrasound too. Norman would put a bit of gel on the probe and move it up and down my shin. When it reached a certain point, the pain was like having another injection. That was a sign of a stress fracture.

I don't know where I got this idea from but I'd go to bed with a pencil taped to my calf underneath the shin bone. That would relieve the pain for a while. The best way to describe it is tricking the tendon further up the shin so that it wouldn't be coming away from the bone. Something like that; I'm a bit confused about it. Someone had explained that, with shin splints, the tendons come away from the bone. In later years you'd see athletes, tennis players, swimmers, all taped up. My pencil was a bit like that. But back in the 80s you'd never see anybody competing with bits of tape stuck all ower them.

With injuries and sometimes with training, if I said to Jimmy I was going to try this or try that, he was the type of person who would say, 'If that's what you want to do, you do it.' Although there were times when he might say that I'd have to take six weeks off or even knock the season on the head.

The problem I had with shin splints was that the first few minutes of the run would be horrendous, but when I got warmed up the pain would go away. If you had a calf strain or a hamstring problem, it wouldn't allow you to run. Shin splints was one of the very few injuries whereby sometimes you could run after warming up. But next day it could be twice as bad.

If I had two weeks off, I might say, right, I'll give it another go tonight. I'd hobble for a few minutes of a six-mile run and then *boosh*, you canna feel a thing. But when I'd cooled down after the run, the same night or the next day I could hardly walk. So that would be another three or four days off. Unfortunately, it left me in the lurch because you might be a week or two away from a major race, and depending on how the injury was, it might allow you to run or it might not. Shin splints weren't there all the time. And that's what the frustrating thing was. Sometimes I'd be thinking, *Great, I've managed ten 400s tonight and I've only been in a little bit of pain.* Two days later it would get to the point when I couldn't even walk. It's an evil injury. You never know whether to have two weeks off or two months off.

Eventually, the only thing to get me over shin splints was more time off. I'd have a good four weeks off doing absolutely nothing. Then I'd come back with ten or 15 minutes of jogging every other night. Then if everything was okay, I'd run ten or 15 minutes every night. Sometimes I'd think, *Great, it's gone.* Then all of a sudden it was back. Nothing much makes me cry, but one night when I got home to my mum and dad's I was in tears. It haunts you.

It's weird because sometimes it would go away as quickly as it came on. The thing is, to run quick 800s I didn't need a lot of training. I'm not saying I'd get fit really quickly but with two or three months of training I could get back down to 1:46. That's how it would seem, that I could run fast with very little training, and that's what happened leading up to the 1988 European

Indoors in Budapest, Hungary, after I'd been injured for a lot of 1987.

* * *

In Budapest I was sharing a room with Paul Edwards, the shot putter. I didn't know this at the time but his nickname was Piggy Edwards. Because of his snoring I don't think I had even one hour's sleep. But I'm almost convinced that had I got a good night's sleep I wouldn't have run any better. I always had a problem waking up in the morning after I'd had a good sleep. I'm not saying I was more prepared because I had no sleep but it certainly didn't affect me one little bit. The human body's a weird thing; it corrects itself. That was only the second time in my career where I ran a race with very little or no sleep the night before. The other time it was my own stupid fault because I had that night on the town with Whitey. But this time it was through no fault of my own.

I lined up for the final of the 800 metres in Budapest with Rob Druppers of the Netherlands and my team-mates, Ikem Billy and Tony Morrell. It was much like a lot of my earlier races at Cosford, both in the way I ran it and that the commentator had to backtrack. The bell had just sounded and he said, 'Druppers, the defending champion, going away.' A couple of seconds later he said, 'Sharpe closing though. The slow early pace has suited him. Can he get in the attack he needs? David Sharpe is running the race of his life. The World Junior champion against the defending European champion. Can Sharpe make it off the bend? And here he goes. And David Sharpe comes home to take the gold medal. What a run that was by the youngster.'

I was European Indoor champion – my first senior international title.

* * *

I usually got on well, having a good indoor season and then a good outdoor season, although people would always say that to have a good summer season you need to get the mileage in the bank in the winter. I couldn't get so much of that in when I was running fast reps for indoor races in the winter, but most seasons I seemed to do well at both.

I had a good indoor season in 1988, followed by an average outdoor season. Maybe it's because I didn't have enough petrol in the tank, as Jimmy would say, or maybe it's because I'd been injured in 1987. But you're never going to be fully fit five or six years in a row.

I ran well in Spain, Morocco, Norway and France, although my fastest was in England: 1:45.98 at the AAAs, which were also the Olympic trials. That was the first chance in my career to qualify for the Olympics, but finishing fourth meant that I didn't get picked. Obviously I was disappointed but after a few days it was like water off a duck's back. Maybe I should have been more bothered. I'd love to have gone to the Olympics and, if I had, I'd probably have run well. But the disappointment didn't last long.

I don't remember much about any of those races. Sometimes I wish I'd kept notes like other athletes do.

* * *

The shin splints came back to haunt me in 1989. The year didn't start well. For some reason there was another European Indoor Championship that year, at The Hague, in the Netherlands. I was defending champion, and I got through my semi-final okay but I didn't even finish in the final. That was obviously a low point. I couldn't wait to get out of The Hague and back to the North East.

Not much else happened race-wise that year. Meanwhile, watching the video of that 1988 European Indoors again and listening to David Coleman's commentary sent shivers down my spine, and still does. It's like reliving the race, one of my best ever.

Although 1989 may have been almost written off, I managed to get back into some consistent training in the winter of 1989/90. I obviously didn't know it at the time but 1990 was going to be a special year.

Chapter Five

Millionaire? I'm Aareet

Jarrow, England and Casablanca,
Morocco, the 80s and 90s

SOME PEOPLE say that I must be a millionaire because I used to run in big races and be on telly. But it wasn't anywhere near £1m and it all went into a trust fund. The most I ever had in mine at any one time was about £20,000. You'd always know how much was in your fund and you were able to draw money out for expenses for warm weather training, special diet, transport, basically anything that helped you with your athletics. But I was never rich, by any means.

I can remember winning an 800 metres race in Casablanca, Morocco in 1988 and going to Said Aouita's house. He was a world and Olympic champion and world record holder, with a huge range from 800 metres to 10000 metres; all pure class. In Nice, in 1985,

Crammy had run 3:29.67 to beat Said and improve Steve Ovett's world record for 1500 metres. Said was only four hundredths of a second behind and also under the old record. They were the first and second athletes ever to run under 3:30, and they were good friends. Casablanca was Said's hometown and he invited Crammy and me to his house for a bite to eat and that. It was a bungalow but it was like a palace: tiled floors, rugs, all traditional Moroccan style. I was living in an ordinary semi-detached house in Jarrow, so to go to Said's house for a spot of lunch and sort of knock about with him for half a day was a big deal. He was a fantastic athlete and a great bloke as well.

I got about $1,000 for that race, which was okay. While I sometimes had a blasé attitude towards training, and had other things going on in my life like the birdwatching and the motorbikes, something that never really bothered me was appearance money. It was the far end of a fart, so to speak.

When Andy Norman came on the scene in the early 80s, he changed the whole thing about how athletes got paid and how much. In the 70s – the era of Brendan Foster, Bedford and Moorcroft – I wouldn't have a clue how much they got, but all of a sudden you had some athletes getting £20,000 a race. How that came about, I don't know for sure, but a lot of it had to do with Andy.

Although we were professional in our approach to athletics, we were classed as amateurs. The golden body was the AAA. Athletics wasn't like football where you might get a signing-on fee and get paid your wages whether you play or not. You had to run races and perform well. And to do that you had to train hard for years.

My relationship with Andy was very good. I probably wouldn't have got into most of those big invitational races without Andy. On the other hand, there were a few occasions when I knew I should have been getting paid more. Andy would say that I was running here or there and was going to get this much money or that much money. How much athletes got paid was a grey area. I never knew what the likes of Tom McKean, Ikem Billy, Rob Harrison, John Gladwin or any of them were paid, and I wasn't bothered. If Andy said I'd get £1,000, that would be it.

I think Andy would start off low and the athlete would negotiate. Although £1,000 for running one race might seem like a lot of money, I'm convinced that if I'd said, 'Right, I don't really think that's fair, I want £2,000,' I'd have got it. But it was never in my nature to ask for more.

One time I was pacing for John Walker and Crammy in the mile. I think it was at the opening of our new track at Monkton Stadium in Jarrow and

I was only about 17. I remember Andy saying to me, 'Right, Sharpey, you're not getting any money but we're going to send you to Australia and New Zealand on a junior international training trip.' Believe me, I knew that I was going on that trip anyway, because I was the best junior at 800m. But basically I just said, 'Right, fair enough.'

It was a month's trip: one week each in Melbourne, Perth, Auckland and Hamilton. A great experience, and I could have had that and the pacemaking money as well, but I just went on the trip.

When Crammy and I travelled to international meets, Crammy would always tell me how the flights were organised and he'd pick me up from my door. But one year when we were meant to be running in Oslo, Crammy got injured and couldn't go. He told me that he'd have been on a direct flight from Newcastle to Oslo, about an hour and a quarter. So I rang the athletics travel agent, only to find out that I was flying from Newcastle to Heathrow, an hour and a quarter in the opposite direction, and then I'd have an hour and a half waiting for a flight to Oslo. So I was like, 'This canna be right, can you book me on the direct flight that Steve Cram was going on?'

'Right, okay, Mr Sharpe. We'll sort that out for you.'

In those days, even people in Jarrow who weren't particularly interested in athletics had heard of Andy

Norman. Whenever he rang me, the receptionist would put it out on the tannoy that he was on the phone. The day before I was due to fly, sure enough, *ding dong* the tannoy went and, 'Andy Norman's on the phone and he doesn't sound happy. He said to tell you to ring straight back and he means *straight back*.'

So I went to reception to ring him back. And do you know what, he was irate.

'WHO THE FUCKEN HELL DO YOU THINK YOU ARE?'

I went, 'What's the matter, like?'

'You're a nobody yet! You've won a couple of races and you think you can do what you like! Just remember, Crammy puts bums on seats and he breaks world records and he flies from Newcastle straight to Oslo. But you were meant to be going down to London then to Oslo and the tickets that we had for you were cheaper. When you break world records, then we'll fly you straight to Oslo.'

I had very few run-ins with Andy but that was one of them. I hadn't known that I'd done anything wrong and even if I had, I thought he'd have just ticked me off, but he went ballistic. That was Andy.

* * *

I had other jobs all throughout my athletics career. Around the same time as I was on the YTS scheme and working in the sawmill or at the welding, I was grateful for a £10,000 award from Northern Rock. Later, when I was training at Monkton Stadium and some local schools were doing their PE lessons there, one of the teachers asked whether I'd come in to their school, have a chat with the kids and show them my medals. Within days of that first school visit, word got around and I got a phone call from another school asking me to visit them, and then another and so on. I'm not joking, within three or four weeks I was inundated.

There was a guy I used to run with who knew one of the leaders at the local council. I didn't know anything about this at first, but he told them a load of bunkum, which helped me. He said that I was going round all these schools, showing them my medals and joining in their PE lessons, all for free. That much was true but he also told them that I'd been approached by the council in Gateshead and that they'd offered to pay me to do the same thing, which wasn't true. He said if that happened it would be a travesty, because I was a South Tyneside lad and I should be doing it in South Tyneside and getting paid for it.

All of a sudden I had this job of sports development officer. (I'd already been on a leisure and recreation course, like.) I wasn't getting paid a great deal but it was a proper contract and it gave me some security. I was based at Monkton Stadium, where schools would bring their kids in for me to take them for PE. I worked for only three or four hours a day but it was something that I enjoyed doing, and it lasted for 30 years. I wasn't bothered how much I got paid, although maybe I should have been, but money was never a motivation for me.

I met Sir Eddie Kulukundis, the philanthropist, around the time of the European Championships in Split in 1990. Sir Eddie gave away millions of pounds to worthy causes and he was a major athletics fan. He asked me how I was doing financially. He wasn't asking directly if I needed any money, but he wanted to know whether I had my own transport. Basically he was asking whether I wanted a car. I told him that I had a car, I was okay. Then he asked about warm weather training and again I said that I was fine. I had an idea what he meant but I didn't want to ask him for anything. He sponsored about ten athletes at that time. He bought cars for them and he paid the mortgage for at least one of them.

But for some strange reason I said, 'No, thanks, I'm aareet.'

When Jimmy heard about it he said, 'You're bliddy stupid, you.'

And I said, 'But I've got a car and I already go on warm weather training. I don't want any more money off anybody.'

I think that some other athletes, if they'd won the races that I won, would have said no, they wanted more. If I got £1,000 for running an international race at Gateshead, only two miles up the road, I'm sure if I'd said, 'No, sling yer hook, I want more,' the majority of people in that stadium would have agreed with me. If it had been elsewhere in the country, it might have been different but it was on my home turf. But I just took what I was given.

Jimmy said I could have got this or I could have got that. And I said, 'I know I could have got it but I didn't, and that's the way it is.'

Sometimes I think maybe I should have accepted Sir Eddie's help or asked for more money for races. But to have had the opportunity and turned it down – that's something I'm quite proud of.

I'm aareet.

Chapter Six:

Split Silver

London, England and Split,
former Yugoslavia, 1990

SOMETIMES PEOPLE can get a person so mixed
up and just wrong. This guy wrote on an online forum
the other day that I was nuts. He said that an hour
before the start of the 800 metres at the 1990 European
Championships in Split, the British team managers
couldn't find me. Apparently I was in the athletes' café,
tucking into a roast dinner. That's absolute bunkum.
As much as I did a lot of things wrong and sometimes
didn't train a lot, I wouldn't be having a big meal an
hour before a major race. I was nuts though.

* * *

What I've noticed about 1990 is that I ran 1:45 for 800
metres six times and 1:46 five times, and had a lot of

firsts and seconds. Whatever I put in that year stayed together. I didn't really have an indoor season in 1990, except one race at 1000 metres in a match against the German Democratic Republic, which I won. I've said before that I loved racing indoors and usually managed to run well outdoors after a season indoors, even though I didn't have the mileage in the tank. But your body can only stand so much.

There was something different about 1990. I'm wondering if not having much of an indoor season, and doing more mileage that winter, is why I had such a good outdoor season and was more consistent, with a string of good races. If I'd run five or six races indoors in January, February or even March, could I have run all those races at a consistent level from May onwards? I don't think so. Jimmy, even though he enjoyed supporting me running indoors, put me in better stead for what happened in the summer.

I ran 16 races: Oslo, Grosseto, Rieti, Belfast, Split, even Bratislava. I can't remember ever being in Bratislava in my life, but I can remember running a one-mile race in Battersea Park, London at the beginning of the season. I ran 3:59 and it nearly killed me. I felt absolutely wiped out. I didn't enjoy it one little bit, although afterwards I was over the moon at breaking four minutes. When I was 16 I'd run 3:46 for 1500 metres and at 17 I ran 3:42, the equivalent of a sub-four-minute mile, which I didn't run until that race in Battersea Park when I was 22. It goes to show what a lazy so-and-so I was about 1500 metres and the mile. I just didn't like running them – going through the half-mile in about 1:59 (which should have felt easy for me) and having all this time to think: *Jesus, I've got another, not one but two laps to go.* For that exact reason I absolutely hated 1500 metres and the mile. Other than the European Championships that year, that mile race at Battersea stands out above the other races in my memory because I hated it so much.

The other thing I remember about that Battersea Park race is that it was the day before the 1990 play-off final at Wembley. Our Lad was Sunderland FC mad. He'd never miss a home match and went to a lot of away fixtures as well. Crammy had a box at Roker Park, and most Saturdays after Jimmy's park session me and Our Lad would go with Crammy to Sunderland's home matches. I wasn't as football daft as Crammy or Our Lad but I got to know some of the players well. Football has completely changed now but back then we'd often have a drink with the players in midweek, only a few days before their matches.

The 1990 play-off final between Sunderland and Swindon was to decide who would be promoted to the top tier (now the Premier League) and we had tickets. When I finished my mile race, knackered and looking forward to a lie-down, I went back to my hotel room, and there, sitting on the bed, was Our Lad. He told me that we were going out to have a pint with George Best. I'd always thought that Bestie was one of the greatest footballers in the world, so it would have been a thrill to meet him, but my reply to Our Lad was that I was too tired and not that bothered about meeting George Best (because I didn't believe him). However, Our Lad persuaded me to go, but when we got to the pub – The Duke of Clarence at Marble Arch – it was closed. I was all for turning back but Our Lad knocked on the door and who should answer but the man himself, who said, 'Oh, Bob, come on in!' How the hell Our Lad got to know George Best in the first place, I've never found out.

I wasn't much of a drinker but I had a few too many that night. It's not every weekend that you have a drink with George Best and watch your team at Wembley, but that's exactly what we did. It should have been a perfect day but I was a bit hungover, Sunderland lost 1-0 and I was ready to go home. I needed to get back to the hotel, collect my stuff and catch a train to Newcastle. But Our Lad said, 'No, we're going to meet the team.' So we ended up bunking up with them at their hotel and travelling up to Sunderland with them the next morning in the team bus.

All this time the players were in full swing. They'd lost their last match of the season and their chance of promotion but you'd think they'd won, the way they were going on. (As it turned out they did get promoted after all because Swindon were demoted due to irregular payments, but the Sunderland players didn't know that at the time.) Well, I was still hungover and a bit worried about the drinking because, although it was the end of their season, it wasn't the end of mine. Anyway, the players and Our Lad kept drinking, but I was fed up because I could have already been home and out running if I'd only caught a train the day before. But I had to follow that bliddy nutter, Our Lad, hadn't I? By this time I'd stopped drinking, and the players were lobbing empty cans at me for being boring. But I'm not joking, I was worried about missing training and mucking up my preparation for the rest of the season.

We left the team hotel at 10 o'clock in the morning and didn't get home until midnight. We must have stopped at every pub between London and Sunderland. And then it was back to training and racing.

* * *

What I loved about 800s was that I never had enough time to get tired. You never even had time to think, especially on the European circuit. As soon as the gun went – *boomf!* – it was almost flat out. The 800 metres had become more or less a sprint. You had the odd tactical race but running 800 metres you never had time to think about being tired. For the same reason I liked the 400 metres too. I rarely ran 400 metres races but I can remember running 47.6 in a time trial at Monkton Stadium.

The good thing about YouTube is that I can watch some of my races from back in the day. Otherwise I always have a problem remembering them. Watching my 800 metres races again, it looks like I'm always struggling to keep up. I could never go through faster than about 52, which is 1:44 pace. There were a lot of races, loads of them on the European circuit, where all these top athletes – Johnny Gray, Benvenuti, James Mays – were going through in 49 or 50 seconds. Now, unless they're going to break the world record, their second lap is going to be at least three seconds slower.

Brendan Foster said to me that everyone was going on about how I was always coming through so quick at the end, from miles off the pace. Commentators moaned, if only I'd make my move earlier. But I was running 52.5 and 52.5, which is 1:45. All these athletes who were going through in 50 seconds – I'm not speeding up, they're slowing down. Brendan said that the art of running a good 800 metres is even pace. But not many athletes did that or learned that. It's something that I'd do, but I wasn't aware of it when I was in the actual race. I wasn't thinking to myself, I'm

72

going to run a 52 and a 52. The truth is that I couldn't run 50 seconds with another lap to run. I'm not saying it was physically impossible but if I'd gone through in 50 seconds, I wouldn't have had my fast finish. Going down the home straight it would have been like pulling up trees. So in all fairness, in a lot of my races it looked like I had a really good kick, which I did, but I wasn't speeding up.

* * *

Oslo, Norway was one of the few places where I'd run three or four years in a row. The Bislett Games were always within a few days of my birthday, 8 July. I got on really well with the promotor, Svein Arne Hansen. Out of all the Grand Prix races in all the countries, Oslo was always on my radar.

For most of the Oslo 800 metres in 1990, I was well behind. Once again the commentator said, 'David Sharpe prefers to hang about at the back.' Well, it was 49.81 for the leader at the bell, so I wasn't going to hang about at the front, like, was I? With 200 metres to go I was still way back, but I came through from about seventh into third place.

'David Sharpe is a latecomer from behind. He's got to do a lot of running.' No surprise there. 'David Sharpe having a spirited run to the line. He's left it late. He always leaves it late.' Okay, okay, I get it. 'Why did Sharpe leave that quite so late? He may have got a personal best out of it, he had a terrific last 200 metres, the Americans were tiring, but oh, if only he'd come a little sooner.'

Johnny Gray and George Kersh were first and second. (Gray had run 13 races under 1:44.) I finished third but it was a race I should have run better. Had I made my move about ten metres earlier, I could have won it. Britain's Steve Heard and Atlee Douglas (who lived in Norway) were behind me. I did run a pb, 1:45.12, and although I didn't get my tactics quite right, it gave me confidence with the European Championships coming up.

The trials were that high a standard that you had to fight really hard to get selected. I finished only fourth, but I got picked. I think it was because I had a record of doing well in major championships. The selection criteria was controversial but it worked for me that year. I was going to Split.

* * *

Frank Dick was British Athletics Director of Coaching at the time and I'll never forget how motivating his team talk was in Split. In fact, it turned out to be a great team performance by Great Britain. We were second in the medal table to East Germany and ahead of the Soviet Union.

I got in touch with Frank recently on social media and after all these years I thanked him. He replied that it was great knowing Jimmy and he'd learned a lot from sitting talking with him. I said that Jimmy would be humbled to know that he was held in such high regard by someone of Frank's stature. I finished by telling Frank how his speech had made me feel confident leading up to the 800 metres final.

Unlike most of my races, when I sat in and sometimes was miles back, I went straight to the front. I remember afterwards the commentator saying it was unusual for me. It's because I knew that the only way I was going to beat Tom McKean and the rest of them – Sudnik from the Soviet Union, Piekarski of Poland, Yugoslavia's Popovic, all great athletes – was at a slow pace, maybe 1:47. So when we broke out of our lanes after the first bend, I went to the front and tried to slow it down. If you watch the video of the race, it stands out like a sore thumb what I was trying to do. Before we got to the second bend, Tom had decided that he was having none of it.

'McKean won't have it,' the commentary went. 'McKean's going to make a race of it. It's not going to just be left to those fast sprinters.' Like me.

Tom went through in 51.31, which, despite me trying to slow it down, was pretty fast. I was hanging on.

'David Sharpe's still with him, really making a bid to hang in there in a fast race. Sharpe's looking strong.'

That was the only race where, as early as 300 metres to go, I was running for second place. I knew that if I kept up that pace, I'd have gone backwards and wouldn't have had a sprint finish. So with that in mind, with about 200 metres left I dropped from second to fifth. And got bumped.

'Sharpe is beaten. Now can McKean win it in the most difficult way possible?'

What the commentator didn't know was that there was a lot of thinking going on. Deliberately slowing down again was the only way I knew that I'd be able to come back a little bit down the home straight. Had I gone with Tom and kept up with him I wouldn't have had that relaxed feeling that I normally had in races. Going through my mind was, if I don't allow myself to tick over, I'll only finish in the top five or six. And that's why I let them go past me at 200 metres. I'd settled for second, while Tom went on to win easily.

'A splendid run by McKean. He's absolutely stormed away, McKean by yards *with Sharpe in second place!*' He was that surprised because he hadn't noticed me sneaking through. 'Sharpe waited for a chance on the inside and when it came he took it. But what a run by Tom McKean.'

Jimmy was over the moon that I'd got silver. However, when I discussed the race with him afterwards, I knew in my own mind that my tactics early on hadn't really worked. At least I'd tried something different. Tom ran a perfect race from start to finish. He certainly wasn't going to let me slow it down. Had he allowed me to control the race at around 54 for the first lap, we'd probably have been neck and neck down the final straight, just like many of our other races, especially indoors.

Tom was a naturally much stronger athlete than me and was happy at 1:44 pace. Whether or not what I did in Split was a good thing or a bad thing, I don't know, but I was pleased with silver. It was like a reward for a really consistent season. And it made me forget all about the shin splints that had haunted me for so long.

* * *

Three weeks before we went to Split, we'd had a letter warning us that the championships might not go ahead, which at the time I didn't understand. Yugoslavia (as it was then) was one of the nicest countries I'd ever been to. Everybody was so welcoming. But within a year or so of the championships, I couldn't believe that the whole country had split and horrendous atrocities were going on so close to where we'd been running. I couldn't understand how that could happen, there and in other parts of the world. It's hard to think about it. I still don't understand. We try to do our best for each other as people. Why can countries not do the same?

Chapter Seven

Crammy

*Around the world, late 80s
and early 90s*

CRAMMY BROKE three world records during a famous 19-day period in 1985: 1500 metres, the mile and 2000 metres. I was watching all this on TV in Jarrow and thinking, *I've got the same coach as this guy and I'm training with him; how lucky and privileged am I?* I hadn't been in the same training group as Crammy that long, but I was finding out that what worked for him also worked for me.

Three times world record holder and world champion, Crammy was already a global star when I started training with him. He did all that whether I was there or not. I was only an up-and-coming athlete. Training and travelling with Crammy was a good thing that led to great things. I owe so much to Jimmy and his coaching, and I'll never know how far I'd have got if it hadn't been for Crammy's help as well. The training and coaching were a massive plus for me.

It was the beginning of not only training and racing but a friendship. I got on like a house on fire with Crammy, although it wasn't like we'd go out at weekends drinking. He had his own group of friends and I had mine. Whatever I did on a weekend – out on the town gallivanting, I suppose – that's something we very rarely did together. We did have the odd night out in Newcastle and I'd go up to his house on New Year's Eve. Sometimes we played golf or snooker. I didn't win many games; I was too erratic, like with anything else I did. Running, motorbikes, cars, birdwatching, golf, snooker, I was always all ower the place. Crammy was more serious and not only a brilliant athlete but a very intelligent person too.

At first we didn't really travel a lot together. Still only 18, I'd run a couple of junior internationals plus England versus USA at Gateshead, but I wasn't good enough to run in Grand Prix meets overseas like Crammy did. We didn't go overseas for training at that time either. But from 1986 onwards we travelled all over the world together for training and racing. There was warm weather training in Australia, at altitude in Denver, Colorado and in other places too. We went to some of the same meets but rarely ran the same event. For instance, one year I ran the 800 metres at the Bislett Games and he ran the Dream Mile.

Jimmy never came abroad when we went for training, but he never missed a session in Jarrow, through rain and snow and all sorts. When I was racing indoors, I'd be doing track sessions outside in January and February in bad weather. Jimmy would be there, week in, week out, most evenings and every Saturday morning for that park session that I hated. But on the warm weather training trips it was only me and Crammy. We'd always tell Jimmy what we had in mind and ask his advice. He understood that there comes a time, when athletes get to a certain age, when they know their bodies and what's good for them.

One of the many good things about Crammy was that he'd give me some great advice but he never tried to get me to do anything I really didn't want to do. In Denver I was struggling with shin splints, Crammy was on his normal 90 miles per week, and I ran nowhere near that. A couple of times on a morning I'd tell him that my shins were too sore, so I'd have to miss the morning run and just train in the afternoon or evening. It was never a case of, 'You've come all the way over here,' or if we were doing 10 x 400 and I dropped out after seven or eight because of pain in my shins, he'd never be pushy and say, 'You need to do this or that.' My mileage must have been half of Crammy's but he never judged me and we never had any disagreements about training.

Not often, but once or twice, our friendship was tested, and it was my fault. One time, when me and Crammy were going to Australia, it was a really bad winter in England, Newcastle Airport was closed and we were worried that we wouldn't catch the connecting flight in London. Eventually we did get there in time and then, 35,000 feet up, when we were sat back and starting to relax after all that panic, Crammy just came out with this: 'At least I've got something to look forward to when we get back. My new car's arriving.'

'Oh? What is it, like?' I asked.

'A Ford Sierra RS Cosworth.'

In those days, that was the car to have. There were only 500 made at the time. I wish he hadn't mentioned it, because I couldn't get it out of my head all the way to Australia, all the time we were there and all the way home. I just couldn't relax. All I could think about was that car.

I don't think Crammy knew how daft I was about cars. I don't think he even knew anything about the car: its horsepower, how fast it could go or that it had been made so that Ford could have a winner in Group A racing in Europe. There was a huge spoiler on the back, basically to keep the bliddy thing on the road, to stop it taking off into the air. But for all that

Crammy won lots of races in Europe, he wouldn't have had a clue.

If someone had asked me, 'What type of car would you like to have, when would you like to have it and what would you give up to have it?' I'd have replied, 'A Ford Sierra RS Cosworth, I'd have it right now. Never mind Australia, I just want the car and I'd give my left arm, left leg or left bollock for it.'

When we got home to Jarrow and back into training, Crammy would drive this car to Monkton Stadium. The car park was outside the gates but, if the gates were open, Crammy would drive the car right up to the clubhouse, where people could keep an eye on it. He was sick of people trying to steal it, even off his driveway. One day he woke up and saw a couple of blokes pushing it down the road to a low-loader down the bottom. That's the type of car it was.

One night the gates were locked and Crammy had to leave his car in the car park. This was one of the times that I was injured but I was down the club that night. Crammy was just setting out for a run with a couple of our club-mates when he realised that he'd left his lights on. He looked back and shouted to me, 'Can you do me a favour and switch the lights off in my car? The keys are in the clubhouse.' Straight away he realised that was the worst thing he could have said

DAVID SHARPE: ENIGMA ON TRACK

to me and he changed his mind: 'No, it's okay, I'll do it when I get back.'

And I said to myself, *No you won't, Crammy. Too late. I've got the keys.* I'm not joking, for me to be sitting in a Ford Sierra RS Cosworth was the best feeling ever. I thought, *This is the best car in the world. I'm sitting in it. Low down in luxury. What shall I do?*

Nothing would have stopped me taking it out that night. I fired it up and off I went, straight down the road to our house to show off to Our Lad. I got up to 70mph in second gear and hammered the bollocks off Crammy's pride and joy. But what I hadn't realised was that Crammy and his mates were running a different route than usual. There was me driving up our street and there was them running down it. I crouched down, trying to hide, which was stupid because the chances of there being another Ford Sierra RS Cosworth on our street were astronomical. Obviously Crammy spotted me and sprinted after me to the car park, where I'd already parked the car and switched the lights off. And where he gave me a right bollocking. Which I deserved. But what a drive.

Another time, in Italy, I had to run an unofficial race before the proper race. I was hanging over my hotel room balcony, and Crammy and a couple of other athletes were directly below in the street. For some reason there was a champagne bucket in my room. It wasn't full of ice or champagne but I filled it up with cold water and doused them all with it from way up above. Why the hell I did this I'll never know, because I got another bollocking off Crammy and the others. When I went down to apologise, one particular athlete (not Crammy) wouldn't let it lie and decided to give chase around the streets of the city. I was quite nervous because I was wondering what he was going to do to me if he caught me. When I came to a dead end I climbed up the wall and drainpipe on to someone's roof. I remember a slate coming off and breaking, and this and that, and obviously one thing led to another, but I got away with it.

After his race, Crammy said if it wasn't for me he'd have won. He said I gave him a head cold or something. I'm sure he was just winding me up. However, drenching everyone with cold water isn't normal behaviour between athletes, so I did always feel a bit guilty. Crammy hadn't run well, I won my race and we were still friends. That says a lot about Crammy.

* * *

There's a story that Crammy tells about me in his after-dinner speeches. It's 100 per cent true. I was looking at the menu in a restaurant in Australia, and asked about the ham and mushroom *kwish*. Crammy looked at me and I looked at him, then the waitress looked at me, and Crammy asked me, '*What* is it you want?' I said it again and Crammy said, 'Give me a look at the menu.' Then he burst out laughing and said, 'It's *quiche*, man.'

To be honest I didn't even know what it was, but I asked, 'Can I have the ham and mushroom *quiche* without the mushrooms?'

The waitress said, 'You can't have it without mushrooms, because it's already made,' and Crammy said the same thing.

'Well,' I went, 'can you not make up another one without mushrooms?'

Crammy's been telling that story at my expense for years but, unless he's reading this book, he doesn't know that I was playing along a bit to make him laugh. I might have been a young lad from Jarrow who had never heard of *quiche* before but even I knew that you can't have ham and mushrooms without mushrooms.

I don't know what it is about me and restaurants, but there's another story too. While me and Crammy were training in Portugal we were invited out for a meal with a restaurant owner. When I got up to go to the toilet, I noticed a huge portrait of a chef. Back at the table, I announced to Crammy, 'There's a big painting of somebody who looks just like this guy sitting with us.'

Well, Crammy just looked at me and I went, 'Ouch!' (He was kicking me under the table.) 'What're you kicking me for?'

Crammy elbowed me and whispered, 'That *is* him. It's Richard Shepherd, the famous chef. I told you this is his restaurant. You never listen, you bliddy nutter.'

* * *

Once, flying back from warm weather training, Crammy's seat was behind mine, and I was sitting next to this older guy, straggly hair, biggish nose, who started talking to me in his cockney accent, really friendly: 'Where you been, what you been doing?'

We chatted for a while, but I forgot to ask him who he was and what he'd been doing, and then I fell asleep. When we got off at Heathrow, Crammy asked, 'Do you not know who that was?'

'No, who was it, like?'

'You haven't got a clue, have you? It was Ronnie Wood from the Stones.'

I've never been a big fan of the Rolling Stones. I might have recognised Mick Jagger, but I had Ronnie Wood sitting next to me for seven hours and I didn't even know. There must be something missing in my musical education. If I'd asked him, he'd probably have told me that he was in the Rolling Stones and they'd just been doing a gig, but as far as I was aware he was just some random bloke on a plane.

* * *

I watched Crammy's races from the sidelines at the Commonwealth Games and Europeans in 1986. His two finals in Edinburgh were like chalk and cheese. He won the 800 metres in 1:43.22, which is still a Games record. The way he did it in those windy conditions was unreal. Then he won the 1500 metres in a slow time but with a really fast finish. At Stuttgart he won bronze in the 800 metres. It looked like he'd lost some of his zest, but he bounced back to win the 1500 metres. And that turned out to be his last major medal. Some people said it was the end of the golden era of British middle-distance running. Whether that's true or not, I don't know.

Crammy was the Jarrow Arrow. Then some wise guy called me the 'Jarrow Sparrow' (Jarra Sparra). I don't know who he was or how he came up with it. Maybe he knew about me and the sparrows in the back garden, or maybe it was my skinny ankles, but the name stuck for years to come. I found it quite funny.

I rarely raced against Crammy, but I did beat him once over 1000 metres in the England versus USA match at Alexander Stadium, Birmingham in 1988. It was a really slow first 600 metres and Tony Morrell was in the lead. Meanwhile, in the commentary box, Steve Ovett was saying that Crammy just wanted to test his speed and that he'd have it over all of us. Then on the last lap he said it was down to who had the best 400 metres speed and that Crammy should still be the one to watch. (Steve Ovett should have known.) Crammy moved up to Tony's shoulder with 300 metres to go, and the other commentator said that I was feeling the pace. But the Jarra Sparra came flying through, late again.

I ran the last lap in 49 seconds, *extricating* myself 'from a very poor position', apparently. I won and it was a 1-2-3 for the North East. The commentator said something about having to review my contract because I'd beaten Crammy, and that I might be in trouble, but I haven't a clue what he was on about.

That was the only time that Crammy was behind me. I don't have a photograph of that race – I wish I had – but I do have one of an 800 metres at Gateshead around the same time, when Crammy won and I was second. He's crossing the finish line and turning round, smiling at me. I don't remember which race came first but it would be nice to think that the 1000 metres was after the 800 metres and I got my own back. It would be the only time, mind.

* * *

When Crammy became more injury-prone towards the finish of his career, that was the beginning of the end of an era for me and Crammy. In all that time we trained, travelled and socialised together, I never had a bad word to say about Crammy. And I still don't.

On the donkey at South Shields 'Fun' Fair. It doesn't look like I was having much fun, does it? (Family)

Our Lad, Mam and me on holiday. Note the bandage on my hand after one of my many childhood pranks (Family)

On the way to winning the 800m at the World Junior Championships, Athens, 1986

Proud to race in my Jarrow & Hebburn vest

Finishing second to Tom McKean in the 1990 European 800m Championship

With Tom McKean after finishing 1-2 in the 1990 European 800m Championship

Starting 800m at the Lean Cuisine Games, Corby, 1992. I went on to win.

Beating Tom McKean and Martin Steele in Birmingham. This is what I call my last decent race.

Taken after one of many training sessions with Jimmy and Crammy at Monkton Stadium. I'm around 17 years old.

One of the few times I raced against Crammy. This was an 800 metres at Gateshead Stadium in the Tyne League

Winter training: 10 x 150 metres with Jimmy in freezing conditions, in preparation for indoor racing!

With Dad at Newcastle Airport after winning the European 800 metres Indoor Championship, 1988. Jackie Charlton, manager of Newcastle United, was on the same flight and mistakenly thought the photographers were there for him!

Indoor 800 metres senior Championship, 1986, which I won as a junior

10K fun run in Middlesbrough

One of very few photos with Jimmy and Mam (second left) at a local presentation. What I love most about this photo is how well Jimmy looks.

Concentrating before the start

A close finish in an 800 metres. No. 48 is Martin Steele (a 1:43 man), 33 Kevin McKay and 32 Jason Lobo

Winning from Ray Browne of the USA, indoors at Cosford

Battered and bruised after my charity boxing match (Family)

Post-retirement weights training in the gym at Monkton Stadium (Family)

With Silke

Chapter Eight

Troubles

Jarrow, England and Belfast,
Northern Ireland, the 90s

I'D READ three or four books about the Troubles in
Northern Ireland. One of them was called *The Shankill
Butchers* about these three guys who would drive around
Belfast, pick up random Catholics and do horrendous
things to them. *Stone Cold* is about Michael Stone, who
lobbed grenades at people at an IRA funeral in Mill
Town Cemetery. Then there were two books about
Robert Nairac, who was in the paras, and went on to go
into IRA pubs undercover. He'd try to get information
about who was in the IRA, and used to get up and
sing 'Danny Boy'. But because of his accent one or
two words in the song didn't come out right, and the
IRA men got him out in the street and jumped him. A
right hard case and a good boxer, Nairac overpowered

a couple of them and grabbed one of their guns before they could take him away and torture him. But the gun wouldn't fire and they killed him anyway. His body has never been found.

I'd also watched the footage of the two corporals who were dragged out of their car and killed in the street. Although it was horrible, I was intrigued about all this stuff. I knew what had been going on when I went to run a race in Belfast. And you won't believe how stupid I was.

After I ran in the Les Jones Memorial in Belfast in 1992, I was the only athlete who wanted to go out for a couple of shandies. I asked the hotel receptionist where the liveliest pub was. She recommended one and told me where it was. So I left the hotel – which was decked in red, white and blue because it was a Loyalist area – and got into a taxi. When I was telling the taxi driver how interested I was in the history of the area, he pulled over and said, 'See that bloke you were on about, Michael Stone? This is the cemetery where the security forces got him. If they hadn't got him, the mob would have lynched him.'

We got back in the taxi, and if I'd been sensible, I'd have asked to be taken back to the hotel. But me being me, I said to carry on to the pub. As I walked in, there were some young lasses standing at the bar, and I went straight up and said, 'Ye aareet, lasses?' They just looked at me and didn't say anything, so I ordered a pint of lager top, like I often did after a run, and sat down on my own. I'd taken a few sips and hadn't even been in there five minutes when a bloke appeared from nowhere and pulled a stool up right in front of me. I'll never forget what he said next.

'Who are ye, what's yer name, where're ye from, and what're ye doin' here?' The way he said it, it was like an interrogation.

I said, 'It's David, I've been running a race, I'm from Jarrow in England, and I'm just having a drink.'

He put his hand out to shake mine and started squeezing it tight, staring at me. 'I'm telling you now,' he said, 'ye've got two minutes to get outta here.'

I'll aways remember the size of his hand wrapped around mine and that his grip literally scared the shite out of me. I knew what he was thinking, it's not rocket science. I didn't have a lot of hair up top and the rest was shaved down the sides. He obviously thought that I was in the army.

I didn't need telling twice. I was out of the pub, into a taxi, away from what must have been a Catholic area, and back into the Loyalist area and the hotel, all within about ten minutes. I was shaking so much that I went straight to bed.

When I woke up in the morning I went down to reception but the woman who had sent me to the pub wasn't there. I told another receptionist what happened and he went, 'Was she mad in the head? What the hell did she send ye there for? What did ye go for? Are you mad as well?'

It brought me back to thinking about what happened to Nairac and all the others. That could have been me. It was the height of the Troubles, and it could have turned out really, really bad for me. People still ask me what was I thinking of. And I always say that I don't actually know why I did it. It was stupid and naive. Even though I'd read all about the history of the place, it wasn't until afterwards that it hit me how dire the outcome could have been. It was a lucky escape. But that was me: a risk taker, acting spontaneously and only thinking about consequences later.

* * *

Back home in Jarrow though, I wasn't so lucky.

Dad used to keep newspaper cuttings of my races, he was that proud of me. But there were other cuttings he kept, which he certainly wasn't proud of, and neither was I.

I was on the wrong side of the law, and it was nothing to do with athletics. In a three- or four-week period I was arrested twice. First of all, there was a bit of a hoo-ha outside a nightclub, and my best mate, Whitey, got arrested. I'm not saying it was because of

Whitey that I got into trouble, but every time I was in trouble with the law, he was with me.

A policeman said to me, 'One more word out of you and you'll be arrested too.' Now then, I didn't say anything bad and I certainly didn't say what they said I said, but it was something like, 'Oh, that's all right then.'

I was grabbed by the arms, put in the back of the police van and charged with 'causing harassment, alarm and distress'. My solicitor said if I agreed to be bound over, it would be only a £50 fine, but I'd have a criminal record. What I said to him was, 'Look, I'm not agreeing to be bound over, and I'm not gonna plead guilty when I didn't do what they're saying I was doing.'

In court there was a police sergeant with 30 years' service and a special constable with 15. My solicitor said that the chances of getting off when I was up against those two were pretty slim. Who was the judge going to believe?

I went, 'Oh no, no, no, I don't want to plead guilty, I want to tell the truth.' So that's what I did. And somehow the judge believed me and threw the charge out completely. I don't know how that happened but I was telling the truth. My card was marked though.

Next there was a headline in the local paper: '"TRACK STAR HIT ME" CLAIM'. I got into a little bit of a scuffle, that's all it was. One night someone was shouting and bawling something at me, which wasn't unusual after I'd become a bit better known on the street. This time I got into a fracas. One thing led to another and I was found guilty of assault, GBH, which went on my record.

I should have left it at that but I appealed. I switched from my local solicitor to a barrister, and went from the Magistrates' court to Newcastle Crown Court, and I lost again. It wasn't a great time in my life.

Crammy was aware of what was going on and he probably thought I was a nutter. But not only did he not judge me when I didn't train as much as he did, but he never judged me about my private life either. What he did say was something like, 'You've just won a big race, it might be a good idea if you started drinking somewhere else, because what happened in Jarrow is going to happen there all the time.'

Jimmy knew about it too, and he was always on my side, no matter what. He knew what type of person I was, and that never in a million years would I go out and deliberately cause trouble. He said I was always going to be a target for jealous people when I was out socialising, and it was something I'd have to try to deal with.

Had I lived in Newcastle, this type of jealousy might never have happened. But if you look on a map, you'll see South Tyneside cocooned by the sea and the rivers Tyne and Wear. Everybody knows everybody's business. Some folk born in South Tyneside never move out of South Tyneside. They're great people, but for every 100 who want to shake your hand, there's always one who will give you a hard time. And that's how I got into trouble with the law.

It's not the only kind of trouble I got into.

* * *

How can I put this? There's another part of my life that got me into hot water – what I got up to on a couple of occasions and how it affected relationships.

One time I was sitting in the back of a bus in Brussels with a bunch of other athletes, including world record holders, not to mention any names. Some of them were taking the mickey out of me, because they'd been to Brussels before and I hadn't.

'Wait until you see this street we're about to pass through,' they said. 'You're gonna see women sitting in windows with red lights on.' They all thought it was a joke, and this, that and the other.

When the bus stopped at the traffic lights (on the red light of course) we did see these women sitting in the windows. Then we turned right, left, and there was the hotel. I can remember thinking that from those traffic lights to the hotel was about 400 metres.

Something that I never did was have a jog the day before a race. I always liked to have a couple of days off. Some athletes would even run early on the day of the race itself. Me: the complete opposite, 48 hours of doing nothing always worked for me. However, arriving in Brussels and seeing the ladies of the night in the windows, I decided to put on my running gear and go for a jog to the red-light zone.

When I got back to the hotel a couple of athletes saw me with my running gear on and said, 'Where you been?'

I replied, 'I've been out for a jog, like.'

To which they replied, 'Oh, out for a jog, were you? Who are you trying to kid? You never jog the day before a race. We know where you've been.'

I replied, 'I'm sure I'm not the only one who goes out for a jog under the lights the night before a race.'

* * *

When I was an athlete and going out in South Tyneside, as well as crossing over to the wrong side of the law occasionally, I'd sometimes attract attention from the opposite sex. Being well known locally, I'd quite happily have a chat with lasses as well as blokes.

If I had a pound for every time a lass touched my leg or felt my bum, I wouldn't be rich, but I'd be a bit better off than I am now. I'm not saying I was bothered – I didn't mind one little bit – but had that been the opposite way round, especially in this day and age, I'd have been in trouble.

Most of the time people approached me because they genuinely wanted to chat about athletics. But some lasses would then go home and twist the story, which made me look bad. And then I was in trouble. I'd get pulled up by the lasses' boyfriends later. Always the same old story: 'You were all over my girlfriend last week,' or whatever. 'She came home and told me. I don't know who the hell you think you are, but back off!'

My long-term girlfriend of the time was very supportive and fully understood that I was going to get this kind of attention. Little did she know what was to come.

After I retired from athletics, something happened that cost me that long-term relationship. I cannot always remember races but this is one of those stories that – hands down – I can remember from start to finish.

A good lad that I knew well asked me for advice because (he said) I was a man of the world. He owned a flat in Heaton and rented it out to two girls. There had been some trouble and a window got smashed. He said he wasn't worried about that, because the girls were going to pay for the damage. But when he'd gone over to sort it out, and they answered the door, they didn't have many clothes on, like see-through nighties with stockings and suspenders underneath.

Well, I knew straight away what was going on in his flat. He was worried that he'd get into trouble for allowing this to happen but he didn't want to kick them out because he needed to keep the rent coming in, so he decided to turn a blind eye. But he didn't know how to tell the girls that.

Now, as he was going away on a long trip and was asking me for advice, I offered to go to his flat to talk to the girls and smooth things over while he was away. So I got their number and rang them up to say I was coming over to keep both sides happy. Which I did do. However, I'd left the bit of paper with their number by our phone at home. So when my girlfriend saw it, she was suspicious. I don't know whether she rang the number or asked someone else to ring it, but she found out what type of place it was. Then everything went shit-shaped.

I must have been good at smoothing things over because – let's just say that the girls were very grateful. But it was a stupid thing for me to do. Understandably, my girlfriend wasn't grateful at all. Not one little bit. She'd been very understanding for 11 years but there's only so much a person can take.

So that was the end of that: 11 years, all gone because of me being stupid. It was my fault, I'm sorry,

I'm not proud of it and I'll never do it again. I may or may not be a man of the world but I've learned through painful experience to understand people's feelings better and treat them with more respect.

And that's the moral of this chapter.

Chapter Nine

World-Beater

Zürich, Switzerland and Havana, Cuba, 1992

THE 1991 track season started with a bang for me when I beat Abdi Bile in an 800 metres race in Crete at the beginning of June. Abdi Bile had won the 1987 World Championships 1500 metres, running 1:46 for the last two laps. He was faster than me at 800 metres and everything else, but he got a shock in Crete because I don't think he'd heard of me.

All I can remember about that race was that the track in Chania was hard and the accommodation, in the basement of a hotel, wasn't great. And that I was obviously fit at the beginning of the season. Running 1:46 and beating Abdi Bile was really promising. I thought that it was going to be another good season because normally what would happen if I ran a fast time that early, things would only get better.

But exactly what happened after that, I cannot remember. For some reason 1991 didn't come to anything. I didn't run much: a couple of 1:47s, finishing fifth, sixth or seventh; that's all. Something went pear-shaped, probably my shins again. If you look at that season, the one before and the one after – had 1991 been a good season that would have been three good ones in a row, which I never experienced at any time in my career.

However, 1992 was a year that came right, mostly. Whatever I did that year obviously worked because I was consistent, a bit like 1990 but even better. I cannot put the success of 1992 down to only one or two things: it was a year when everything came together.

I didn't have an indoor season in 1992, so that might be why I ran so well outdoors. But I don't think my mileage was much higher that winter, even without the track sessions to prepare for indoor races. I did go through stages of running higher (for me) mileage but I cannot remember if I did it that winter. I didn't like training twice a day, although maybe I should have done. But sometimes I gave it a go to get my mileage up, and now and again I reached 60 or 70 miles per week, even once getting up into the high 70s. But it never agreed with me. I was always worried about my shins. Maybe the shin splints were an indication that high mileage wasn't for me.

Or maybe it was just that I was lazy. I'd always struggle to go for a run in the morning. When I think about it, sometimes I'd do only about 25 or 30 miles per week. Yet I managed to run the times I ran despite that very low training mileage.

* * *

I see from Power of 10 that I ran 1:45.93 for second place in Verona on 17 June. But if anyone was to ask me what I remember about Verona, I'd have to say, 'Nothing at all.' (No surprise there then.) But obviously it was a fast time so early in the season.

At the end of that month, I ran even faster (1:45.61) at the Olympic trials (the AAAs) in Birmingham, but I must have got the race wrong because I didn't get picked. The top three – Curtis Robb, Steve Heard and Tom McKean – all went. The reason I didn't get selected was that I didn't finish in the first two, or first three for that matter. I was fourth. I probably hadn't learned any lessons from the 1988 trials when the same thing had happened.

I was disappointed at finishing fourth because that was the end of my chances of being selected for the Olympics. But I've always believed that if I tried my best in a race and it was the best I could do on the day, I shouldn't be too down in the dumps if I didn't win or get picked. It wasn't the be-all and end-all, and the disappointment probably lasted only a day or two. Maybe it should have been another kick up the backside, but I wasn't absolutely devastated.

Despite those early season fast times, it looked like, at the time of the trials, I was a few weeks behind where I should have been, like I mistimed my fitness. Had I been as fit at the end of June as I was to be in August, I might have been chosen and gone to the Olympics. Then who knows what might have happened? Nobody knows and none of us will ever know.

Anyway, that was that. I wasn't going to the Olympics, so I had to refocus.

Two weeks after the trials, and three weeks before the Olympics, I ran 1:45.25, another season's best, at Crystal Palace. Kiprotich of Kenya won in 1:44.94 from Tom McKean, who was only a hundredth of a second in front of me. The other two athletes who had beaten me at the trials – Steve Heard and Curtis Robb – were behind me. So my tactics, as well as my times, were improving. A week later, I won at Gateshead in 1:45.09, a pb. This time I beat Tom as well as Steve. Maybe they were thinking about the Olympics coming up in a fortnight's time, I don't know.

I often had a bit of a problem not knowing how fit I was. Around the time that Tom, Steve, Curtis and all the others were on the start line at the Olympics, I was lining up at the back in a 5K handicap training run on the roads around Jarrow. I ran well under 15 minutes, which might be a bread-and-butter time for distance runners but was unusual for me. I'd love to know how accurate the course was; I feel like going back and measuring it. Surprisingly, that 5K road run helped to set me up for some good runs over 800 metres.

When everyone else was at the Olympics, my training didn't change much from what I'd done in previous years. My 10 x 300 metres and 10 x 400 metres and stuff. Sunday long run (usually ten miles); Monday seven miles; Tuesday track session; Wednesday road run; Thursday track session; Friday off; race Saturday. On numerous occasions, like when I had more than one race, I'd have two or even three days off in a week. So sometimes training only four or five days a week. I suppose I was being a bit lazy.

But the track sessions were hard and fast. One of my best-ever sessions of 10 x 400 metres was round about the time of the Olympics that year. I was training on my own, which was unusual because there was usually a group of at least five or six of us. I think I averaged 59 seconds for the first seven or eight and ran the last two or three a little bit quicker. Normally, even when there was a large group including Crammy and a few other good lads, I'd start off running 61s, but on this occasion I was surprised that I was banging out 59s. The recovery between each rep was a minute. Jimmy would always say that the times you ran were important and you had to try to average a similar time for each rep, but the most important thing was a strict recovery time.

It was an indication that I was really fit.

* * *

A fortnight after the Olympics I won in 1:46.03 at Don Valley in Sheffield and beat all three GB Olympic 800 metres runners. Maybe they were tired after the Olympics; that's for others to say but I knew that I was coming into some good form.

Five days later, on 19 August in Zürich, Switzerland, I was lining up in the 800 metres at the Weltklasse meeting.

When you run 1:45 for 800 metres it's always going to be hard trying to improve, and you could hover around a time like that for years. If you look at our top 800 metres runners of that era, you'll see a similar pattern. Tom McKean, Ikem Billy, Brian Whittle, Steve Heard, myself and many more would always be around the 1:45 mark. It would only be the likes of Crammy and Coe who would bang out the odd 1:42 and even world records, which made them a cut above the rest. Leading up to Zürich I felt something good was coming but in all fairness I had no idea how fast it would be.

I can certainly remember how the race went in Zürich because I've watched it loads of times on VHS. I was actually in the 'B' race. I've no idea why. With 300 metres to go I was still near the back. In the video I'm actually out of the picture. I've never worked out how the hell I won it from there. When I hit the front with about 150 metres to go, I took about ten metres out of the whole field and won by a big distance. Steve Heard was runner-up, almost a full second behind.

When I crossed the line and looked at the time I thought, *Jesus! I canna believe I've just run 1:43.98.* It's unusual for an 800 metres athlete to knock a second and a bit off their pb. I hadn't even run 1:44 before that race, although I had run a shade over the 1:45 mark. I knew I was fit but I didn't think I was ever going to be in 1:43 shape.

That 1:43.98 could easily have been 1:44.02. I was over the moon to dip under 1:44. Those two or three hundredths of a second are unbelievably important. To be able to say '1:43–something' instead of '1:44–something' makes a huge difference. Of all the races I won – the World Juniors, the European Indoors and the rest of them – one of the things that always sticks in my mind is running 1:43. It's something I'm proud of. At the time only a handful of British athletes had run that fast. I found out later that it was the fastest time by a UK runner that year. By the way, William Tanui, the Olympic champion, won the 'A' race in an identical time.

A strange thing about Zürich was that after the race Andy Norman and I got on the bus and he told me about all the races he'd set up for me for the following year, 1993. He said, 'Right, Sharpey, this is what's going to happen next year.'

I've said before that I didn't get paid much for races, maybe £1,000 or sometimes £2,000. But that 1:43 struck a chord in Andy's brain, and suddenly I had offers of £3,000 to £5,000 per race, for races in a year's time. The more I think about it, what surprised me was that Andy was basing this 1993 series purely on a time: that 1:43. It was like I was now his new protégé.

It was a far cry from that day he phoned me up at Monkton Stadium and shouted that I was a nobody.

Nine days after Zürich I ran 1:45 for third in Brussels, and I beat Tom McKean and Curtis Robb again. Then three days later, on the last day of August, I was in Belfast at the Les Jones Memorial. Curtis Robb, who had been selected to go to the World Cup in September, was also in my race, the 1000 metres. Well, I won in a fast time of 2:17.79, another pb. Suddenly Curtis wasn't going to the World Cup; I was. I don't know whether Curtis relinquished his place to let me go, but I'm almost sure that it must have been up to him to say if he didn't want to go. Because you don't get selected and then deselected, do you?

From Northern Ireland I went on to Italy for a couple of races. I was only eighth in Turin in 1:47.05, my slowest time of the season. Tom beat me in that one, but two days later in Rieti I ran my second-fastest 800 metres ever: 1:44.67 for fourth, and beat Tom again.

And then there was only one race left: the World Cup, in Havana, Cuba on 25 September.

* * *

Before we went to Cuba, the GB team had a week in the Bahamas, which was absolutely fantastic.

One day I suggested that me, Colin Jackson, John Regis and a couple of others rented out some jet skis. Which we did do. Now then, as far as I remember, Colin Jackson's jet ski crashed into John Regis and hurt his ribs. So John was injured, couldn't run, and Linford Christie, who also ran the 100 metres, took his place. I was aareet though.

I went into the race thinking that I could win it. Again I was way down at the bell and even into the back straight. I was all ower the shop in the home straight, weaving in and out. If a gap hadn't opened up – and it was *nothing* – I'd never have been able to thread my way through. It shouldn't have happened but I squeezed into a tiny space in the middle and won by less than a tenth of a second in 1:46.06. Tanui was second and Benvenuti third. Barbosa, who had led most of the way, was fourth.

The commentator (as usual) kept going on about how far back I was and how I shouldn't be giving too much ground to athletes of that calibre. But, immediately after the race, Brendan Foster made that comment about how the others ran 52 and 54 or slower, but I ran two 53s: even pace.

Because it was called the World Cup, a lot of people who aren't really that genned up on athletics thought it was as good as the Olympics or the World Championships. But it wasn't such a big deal in athletics, not like the football World Cup. It's like, what's in a name? To be honest, with the World Cup being at the end of the season, I don't know how much those who had been to the Olympics put into it or how much training they did between the Olympics and the World Cup. Obviously I'd kept on training. I was inclined to say that maybe I won it because the others were tired after the Olympics and they weren't that bothered. You often find that athletes who've won the Olympics – anything after that, they've lost a bit of fitness and, I suppose, interest.

All the same, I was over the moon to win. To come away with a 1:43 and a World Cup win, and beat the

Olympic champion and others who were in the 800 metres final made 1992 a fantastic season. Had I gone to the Olympics I don't think I'd have been any better known. I'm not saying it was irrelevant that I didn't make the Olympics but I was almost relieved that the whole scenario of not being there was now water under the bridge. Quite honestly it was neither here nor there. For me, the 1:43 and the World Cup win made up quite a bit for not going to the Olympics. Had I gone, and got a medal, it would have been different. But no one remembers who finishes seventh in their heat or something like that. I like to think that those that do remember me at all remember me for winning the World Cup.

Me and Jimmy would often review races as they happened rather than discuss the whole season. Whatever Jimmy had to say was taken in steps. After each race he'd say something like, 'Bliddy good run, that. Fantastic time, unbelievable,' or, 'Do you know that you've just beaten the Olympic champion? Well done, brilliant.'

But I'll certainly always remember all that I achieved in 1992. What next? I was looking forward to 1993 and that series of races that Andy Norman had lined up for me.

Chapter Ten

Retirement

Jarrow, 1993–1995

I DIDN'T wake up one morning and decide to retire. It happened gradually over more than a year.

I started 1993 off promisingly with a good indoor season. There was a match in Glasgow against Russia at the end of January, when Tom McKean beat me in a close race. And then three weeks later in Birmingham, I beat Tom and Martin Steele. The lead changed hands several times, even in the short home straight, and I came through with a trademark late finish to win. Obviously I didn't know it at the time but that was my last-ever good race.

It's hard to pinpoint what went wrong in 1993 after running those two really good indoor races. I don't think it was because I was doing winter track sessions instead of mileage. I'd done that before and had a good outdoor season. So I don't know. But compared with 1992 it was a very disappointing season.

Andy had all those races lined up for me but I ended up going to only a few of them. It wasn't that I'd decided not to go. Our unofficial agreement had been subject to me running quickly enough to be invited. But it all fell by the wayside early on in the season. Nice, Zürich, Cologne, Monte Carlo or wherever – never happened.

I've always said that I was never bothered much about what I got paid. But I remember thinking at the time that the £3,000 to £5,000 a race could have been a total of £30,000 to £50,000 by the end of the season. Had I started the summer of 1993 like I finished the autumn of 1992, that unofficial contract would still have been up and running. But that's the way athletics works, unfortunately so for me.

There was a 4 x 800 metres relay in Portsmouth early in June. I can see from the results that our team's time was 7:12.66 – an average of just over 1:48 per runner (I don't know what my split was but I'm sure it wasn't very good) – and we came third. All I remember about that race is that it was a long way to go for a relay that didn't mean anything. My fastest time that season was 1:46, which wasn't too bad, and my slowest was 1:49, which was. I don't think I won any races outdoors in 1993.

It obviously wasn't good that I was running so slowly. On the other hand it boils down to this: how bothered was I? Was I disappointed? Probably yes. Was I bothered as much as I should have been? Probably not. Was it the be-all and end-all? No, it wasn't. And that was me down to a T.

Had I been more focused it might have been different. But I always had this attitude that whether I ran great or I ran bad – if I'd tried my hardest, that was okay. At the end of that poor season, it didn't bother me that much, no. It should have done. Maybe that was the problem, maybe I should have been bothered a lot more. But it wasn't everything to me. Looking back, I did as much as I could to prepare for the 1993 season as I did for 1992. I was coming up to eight or nine years of competing. Some years went well – great. The years that didn't go well – so be it. It's like, okay, they didn't work out but I've tried my best.

Jimmy didn't say a great deal about 1993. He might have told me that I could have done better but, probably the same as me, he couldn't pinpoint why things were going wrong. I was training day in, day out, week in, week out, month in, month out, but it just wasn't going right for me. Although Jimmy would say that he had a magic wand, that would only happen in really good years. But when I had a bad year, me and Jimmy would chat but neither of us knew the reason.

Some coaches are strict with their athletes and say, 'You're going to do this and you're going to do that and if you don't turn up, that's you and me finished.' Not Jimmy. He certainly wouldn't say, 'Look, you need to buck your ideas up, you haven't done this, you haven't done that.' Jimmy was quite soft when it came to things like telling me I should be doing more. Deep down though, I knew that I should be doing more training.

Jimmy would always say, 'I'll see you at 10 o'clock Saturday morning.' (One of my old club-mates reminded me recently that Jimmy would tell him to knock on my door to make sure I was out of bed for the park session.) But even if on the odd occasion I didn't turn up or I was a bit wild, Jimmy would never say a wrong word to me or have a wrong word said about me.

Jimmy and I had something special. We were more than coach and athlete. Jimmy would never give me a bollocking or say anything that might jeopardise our relationship and friendship. He'd lower his voice and say something like, 'Right, me bonny lad, I think you could have run a bit better,' or, 'What happened to you on Saturday morning?' They'd be just little friendly reminders that he might not have been happy about the way I was going on. And that's exactly the way he was.

Over all those years I don't think we ever said a wrong word to each other. Except once, when Jimmy took the huff. It wasn't about athletics: it was golf. Jimmy loved his golf. We used to play together, but one time me, Crammy and one or two others went to play without Jimmy.

I went into the clubhouse the next night and Jimmy said, 'Enjoy your game of golf on Monday, did you?'

'Oh, aye, em ... Aye, aye.'

'Did you not think about ringing me?'

That's the only time I ever saw Jimmy rattled (although in a nice way).

* * *

The only season that I missed out completely was 1994. I knew all about shin splints, how they'd be painful one day, then the pain would disappear and come back. My Achilles tendon injury was different. It was a build-up of scar tissue. The tendon on my left foot was swollen; it looked about twice the size as the right. I didn't know how to deal with it. I remember trying to run through the pain, then resting and icing the tendon, but nothing seemed to work. Months later, the last resort was an operation to have it scraped.

After surgery, I was in plaster for six weeks or more, and ended up with a four- or five-inch scar. Once the plaster came off, I was stretching and doing strength exercises to build up the muscles in the left leg that had wasted while they were in plaster. Then light jogging, then a ten-minute run every other day. And eventually some track work.

It was an exciting time because I thought, or hoped, that I was fixed and could get back to doing what I loved. By then it was 1995.

At first I must have been doing something right because I got invited to a race in France. However, I was fourth in 1:51, my slowest time for absolutely ages. I had one more race in Gateshead but I dropped out. I think it was only the second time that I'd failed to finish a race. Why did it have to be on my home turf?

And that was it for the 1995 season. I'd broken down. The operation hadn't worked.

I was more than a little bit peed off but even in 1996 I was still thinking that all I needed was a couple of months of decent training, and I could run 1:47, which might have been good enough to go on and do things. I knew I'd never get back to running 1:43, mind.

Around that time, *The Independent* newspaper interviewed me for an article called 'Life Without Your Profession'. Apparently, when I was making the journalist a cup of tea, I was humming 'What Becomes of the Brokenhearted', which he thought was quite apt, because I was trying unsuccessfully to come back into athletics, and maybe feeling sad and missing what I loved to do.

I was also thinking about retirement. I was only 29.

There was no announcement that I was retiring; I just faded off the scene. But, as you know by now, I never ate, drank or slept athletics.

Chapter Eleven

Wild Child Again

Jarrow, 1996 and the 2000s

WHILE I was in athletics, although I had a colourful life, there were some things that I wanted to do but never did, because of being an athlete. So when I retired I went apeshit, a bit like when I was a kid.

The trouble I got into after only a few months of retirement was ridiculous. I was clarting about again, reliving my childhood. It was like I was unleashed to do all the things I couldn't do while I was competing. And now I could. *Boosh!* It was madness. I was that wild child again.

First there were motorbikes. Way back, I'd had a little 50cc motorbike when I first started running. Around that time Jimmy was interviewed about Crammy and coaching. The journalist asked Jimmy whether there were any other of his athletes they should look out for. Jimmy said there was one (me) who was promising, and the best thing that he (me) had done so far was to get rid of his bliddy motorbike, which Jimmy had 'suggested' that I did.

Now that I'd retired and knew that I probably wasn't going to run again, I couldn't get back on a bike quickly enough. I bought a ZXR400, my first big bike. I went on to get a 600cc and then a 1,000cc. Even the 400cc could get up to 140mph. (I got 144mph out of mine, by the way.) If an athletics Grand Prix and a motorbike Grand Prix were on the telly at the same time, I'd be watching the motorbikes.

If there was ever a case when I was a bit of an arsehole back in the day, I could pick any one from a whole series of arsehole stories about me on motorbikes. The way I used to ride, I was an absolute pillock. Not thinking about other road users or my own safety, it was all about this zest for speed again. I was 30 years old and hadn't grown up. I don't know whether it was because I was missing athletics, but I still had a *need* for speed.

Within a few weeks of getting back on the bike, I wanted to do a slider, which is getting your knee down when you're leaning over to go round a corner. Unless you've got loads of experience, one of the stupidest things you can do is to get your slider to touch the ground, especially when it's cold and wet. Guess who tried it in the rain? That's when I ended up covered in mud in a farmer's field. But a bit of mud wasn't enough to put me off.

One day I was flying down the road near the King George Leisure Centre in South Shields. It was a 30mph limit and I must have been doing at least double that. I hadn't noticed this copper with his motorbike parked behind the bus stop – until he popped out and pointed his speed-detector gun at me. I didn't even have time to stop for him, I was going that quick. So I went down to a roundabout about 300 metres away, and came back up the other side, then pulled up alongside the copper, who gave me a bit of a bollocking. Which I deserved.

However, luckily for me, he said, 'Look, if you want to ride like an idiot and kill yourself, that's up to you. But we're right next to a bus stop and the sports centre. What if a kid had run out? There's tracks where you can ride at speed but not here. Look, I've got a motorbike myself, and on this occasion I'm going to let you off with a warning. Just get a grip, screw your head on right and think about what you're doing. Right, bugger off, I don't want to see you riding like that again.'

Two or three weeks later me and my mates were getting ready to go to a race day at the track in Knockhill, just over the Forth Road Bridge in Scotland. We met at 10 o'clock at the house of the guy who had organised it, and he said, 'Look, Sharpey, we'll all have to be careful and stick to the speed limit (within reason) on the way up because we're waiting on a guy coming with us. He's a canny bloke but he's a traffic cop.'

Guess which traffic cop it was? We took our helmets off and looked at each other. I didn't know what to do. I think I just said, 'Are ye aareet?' and he said, 'Aye.' I don't know whether him coming was a coincidence after him giving me a ticking off, but it was a pretty tame journey up to Knockhill that day. And I did behave myself. Until we got to the track. Because even after that friendly warning from the traffic cop, I was still the daftest of us.

Another time, the police followed me and my mates on our motorbikes for 15 miles. When they eventually caught up with us they pulled us over for dangerous driving.

My solicitor wanted to do a deal with the police so that we'd plead guilty to careless driving, not dangerous driving. But the police wouldn't have it, and at Hexham Magistrates' we all got a year's ban. That was a big worry for me, because it was a ban from *all* driving, which meant that I couldn't drive kids around in the minibus as part of my job with the council.

The police said that I couldn't possibly have seen anything approaching from the opposite direction when I was riding at that speed round the bends. But I went back to the scene and took photos and, to cut a long story short, my solicitor appealed successfully at Newcastle Crown Court and proved that I had a clear view of the bend and could have easily seen anything coming. She had experience as a pillion passenger, so she knew about riding on bends and what you could or couldn't see. So the charge was reduced and I walked away with six points on my licence instead of a ban for dangerous driving. I was relieved that I could still drive, especially for work.

* * *

I met my partner, Silke, at a charity night in a club. She was dressed as Pippi Longstocking. I'm six foot but Silke's taller than me, and she had Doc Martens on as well. She was head and shoulders above every other woman in the nightclub – easy to spot – so I made my way over to her and asked how she was doing. The way she answered, I was trying to work out where her accent was from. She sounded like Arnold Schwarzenegger, so I thought she was Austrian. Especially when she was about to go to the toilet, and said, 'I'll be back.' Which I thought was hilarious. (Silke's from Germany, by the way.)

When I asked her if I could take her out, she said, *'Auf keinen fall.'* (No we-ah.)

Later on though, I did take her out, on the back of the bike. Now, there's nothing worse than somebody being on the back of your bike. It spoils your whole day. And with me riding, it's not much fun for the passenger either. Most of them would say, 'You're a bliddy lunatic. Never again!'

But Silke said, 'I loved that! When are we going out again?' How it didn't scare the living daylights out of her, I'll never know. Silke is the only person who would ever go out on the back of a bike with me. And the only one to put up with me all these years.

* * *

Throughout my career I sometimes thought about how successful I might have been in another sport. It's no secret that given the opportunity I'd have jumped at the chance of being a rally driver or a motorbike racer or whatever.

I'd also thought about boxing. It's something that I've always enjoyed watching. Not long after I retired from athletics, a mate of mine booked a table for ten people at a charity boxing night. The table cost £250, which would all go to the charity. My mate asked me whether I'd represent the table at white collar boxing (for people who hadn't boxed before), and I said that aye, I would.

For about eight weeks leading up to the event I did some boxing training, which I found really hard. It was a completely different type of fitness from running.

Only the second time I went, the coach put me in the ring for a bit of sparring with a young up-and-coming boxer. This lad was only about 16 (and I was into my 30s) but within a couple of minutes he knocked me straight on to my arse.

On to the charity night, this big, thick-set guy, nicknamed 'Hally', approached me and told me that he was the one who would be fighting me.

'Is that what you're wearing?' he asked.

I was like, 'What do you mean?' (I was wearing running shorts and training shoes.)

'Have you got no boxing shorts or boots?'

'Well, no. I've never boxed before.'

I didn't know how important it was to have the right footwear. When he asked me if I wanted to borrow his old boxing boots, something didn't ring true because none of us was supposed to have boxed before.

When I walked out into the ring, it was surrounded by noisy folk at their tables, all full. Except ours, which was empty. None of my mates had turned up but Hally's had. When I got into the ring they were all laughing about how short my shorts were, and chanting: 'He's even had a sunbed! He's even had a sunbed!'

There were three rounds of three minutes each. I got bashed about a bit and lost the first round, although I did manage to throw a couple of punches. The referee was Graeme Ahmed, who had boxed against Nigel

Benn in the 80s. Between the first two rounds he told me that I was doing really well and he gave me a tip about jabbing with my right and swapping my feet around. With that advice I did a lot better in the second round and then I actually won the third. The end result was a draw.

Even though I'd trained for eight weeks, that bout was one of the hardest things I've ever done. How could nine minutes be so difficult? I was absolutely knackered. The last round couldn't finish early enough for me. I'll never do it again. There weren't many marks on Hally but I had a big shiner. You should see the photo.

A couple of months later, I went along as a guest to present some trophies at a local boxing match. And who was top of the bill? Hally. And he was supposed to never have boxed before. Not only that but he won the match. And I was thinking, *I drew with this guy.*

* * *

Skiing was something else that I had a mad interest in and had always wanted to do. My first skiing holiday was in Andorra with a mate who had been there before. First of all we went along to practise on the dry ski slope in Sunderland, where there are three or four starting points, from one about 30 metres from the bottom, right up to one at the top.

So which one did I come down from straight away? The top. I crashed into some mats and bent my thumb right back. I thought I'd broken it (I still cannot use it properly to this day). So that was the end of my trial run. Which was nothing like the real thing.

When we got to Andorra, I took to skiing like a duck to water. I loved the speed and I was an absolute lunatic. On the first day I learned to weave from side to side and use the poles. Sometimes I even did without them. But what I didn't learn properly was how to stop. It was bedlam.

While I was being an idiot, I clipped an edge (hit a rough bit) and crashed again. I don't know whether I'd done the shoes up too tightly or what, but the shoes stayed stuck in the skis, the skis stayed stuck in the snow and I twisted my knee.

That was the end of my skiing for that trip. It was a seven-day holiday and I spent six of them doing nothing. But it didn't put me off (or I didn't learn my lesson) because I went back every year for ten years. And I did learn how to stop.

But I was still going too fast. Whether it was on the motorbike, in a car or on skis, I was never worried about getting injured. Nothing would stop me from going as fast as I possibly could. Whatever I was doing, it had to be fast. Even nowadays, everything has to be done in a hurry.

* * *

On the other hand, my interest in fishing was more sedate and came quite late. Silke and I were renting a remote cottage in the Highlands, where we were the only ones who didn't fish. So I thought I'd give it a go and bought a rod, hooks, weights and this, that and the other. I also borrowed a book about fishing but no one taught me how to cast out. When I tried it, the weight would come flying past my head. One time I hooked my hat off.

Another time the hook ripped my brand-new tracksuit bottoms. I thought, this isn't for me, I'm gonna end up bliddy killing myself.

However, when we got home from the holiday I decided I'd continue fishing and go down to the Tyne in Jarrow.

Although I wasn't catching a great deal, I enjoyed fishing because it tied in with some of my other interests, which weren't always about speed. Since I was a kid, I'd always been interested in birdwatching and photography. Now I was discovering that fishing gave me an opportunity to encounter other wildlife. One time I left my rod set up and went for a walk along the riverbank with my owl-caller. When I got back there was a fox in the back of the car, eating my bait. I loved foxes, especially this one because I ended up being able to hand-feed it.

I could also hear seals in the river; it sounded a bit like whales surfacing. On another occasion I saw an otter. At first I thought it was a cat until it slunk into the water and popped back up.

A bird that's extremely elusive and hard to photograph is the kingfisher. This would be my next challenge. I stuck a branch in the middle of a bucket full of cement. When the cement had hardened I placed the bucket, with only the branch showing above the water, in the middle of the river. Then I waited with my camera set up. I knew there was a kingfisher nearby, so when I heard its sharp *tweet-tweet-tweet*, I was ready to look out for its flight path. Its turquoise wings whirred like mad as it swept low and straight across the water and it really looked like it knew where it was going. My branch! So now I've got a photograph of this beautiful bird on my branch, with its huge bill that looks too big for its dumpy body; brilliant orange breast; white cheeks; and red feet. The homemade perch certainly worked and after a two-hour wait I'd been rewarded. To this day it's one of my favourite photos.

I'd come home to Silke after fishing and she'd ask me whether I'd caught anything. I'd reply, 'No, but I've heard owls and seals, seen an otter, made friends with a fox and photographed a kingfisher.'

My mate, Stewy, asked me once whether we could go fishing together, but I said I couldn't until I knew what I was doing. 'Stewy, if one of those weights came flying past and hit you on the head, or if I hooked your face or something, I'd never forgive myself.'

Well, I don't think I've ever really known what I was doing, so I've always gone fishing on my own, in case I cause anybody an injury. I'm honestly not bothered if I don't catch anything. I enjoy the peace and quiet, meeting wildlife, and not rushing around at 100 miles an hour like I usually do.

However, sometimes I just cannot help myself. You'd think at this tender age of 55 my accidents would have slowed down, but when you've been used to speed, it's hard to shake it off.

During a cold snap I went to work on a scooter and nearly killed myself on some ice. Which is no surprise. Hey, I'm not joking, the front end of the scooter just slid away and I ended up on all fours, arms spread out. I'm as accident-prone now as I was when I was a kid. And just like back then, it was my own fault. I shouldn't have been using a scooter, like – with ice here, there and everywhere. But that's the way it goes, I suppose.

* * *

Silke and I used to go away in a caravan. I'm calling it caravanning – I'd obviously sleep in the van but, other than that, Silke wouldn't see much of me. As soon as we hooked the van up, I'd be away all day. Caravanning was a way of getting to wild places where I'd see eagles or other wildlife. Excited about being out in the middle of nowhere, I was driven by the thought of what I might see. The anticipation of spotting a deer or a falcon. The buzz when they appear. And then the photographs I took and will always have. And always remember.

Although I've got a short attention span and can't keep still for long, it's different with wildlife. The ultimate anticipation is waiting for an eagle to fly into its eyrie, even when I've been sitting still for hours on end. Sometimes people ask me where the best place is to see eagles and what's the best way to go about it. My reply is this: 'To see an eagle, you don't just walk up the glen. You have to become part of the glen.' This could mean spending six or seven hours waiting for an eagle to appear. Sometimes you'll see absolutely nothing at all. However, it did lead on many occasions to finding their eyries.

Now *that* is as exciting as speeding on a motorbike or down a ski slope. Or running fast on the track.

A young golden eagle chick on its eyrie on the Isle Of Arran; photo taken from only about 20 feet away (David Sharpe)

The elusive kingfisher sitting on my home-made perch; one of the best photos I've ever taken (David Sharpe)

Sharpe misses court

INTERNATIONAL track star David Sharpe failed to appear in court today - because of a running engagement in Turin.

Sharpe, 25, of Roman Road, Jarrow, is accused of assault occasioning actual bodily harm.

He failed for the second time to appear before South Tyneside magistrates at Hebburn.

The court was told Sharpe could not attend because he was taking part in a Grand Prix meeting in Turin tonight, where he is due to run in the 800 metres.

Philip Cordery, defending, successfully applied for the case to be adjourned to Hebburn Magistrates Court on September 11. Sharpe was granted unconditional bail.

He said: "David Sharpe is running for his country and is unable to attend court today."

The adjournment was not opposed by Dennis Scully for the Crown Prosecution Service.

'Sharpe Misses Court' (news clipping, 1992)

RELIEVED RUNNER TO CONCENTRATE ON OLYMPIC GAMES

Champ cleared over police clash

■ **Cleared:** Athlete David Sharpe yesterday.

CHAMPION athlete David Sharpe was cleared of a charge arising from a clash with police who arrested his drinking partner.

Police said Sharpe caused a disturbance in the street when officers tried to arrest a friend for drunkenness.

But South Shields magistrates yesterday cleared the European 800m silver medallist of behaviour likely to cause harassment, alarm, or distress.

Sharpe, who trains with World mile record holder Steve Cram, said after the case he was ready to put it behind him and concentrate on this summer's Barcelona Olympics.

The runner, 24, was arrested early on Sunday, April 4, outside Victor's Nightclub, South Shields.

Sharpe, of Roman Road, Jarrow, said after the case he would be glad to forget it.

"I'm very relieved it's all over," he said.

By JANE PIKETT

"The whole thing has been hanging over me since April. I considered agreeing to a binding over to get the case dropped but I would still have had a criminal record. I could not have lived with that.

"I am not a criminal and my

> **QUOTE**
>
> ❝ I am not a criminal and my behaviour on that night was nothing to be ashamed of. ❞
>
> **– DAVID SHARPE**
> 800m medalist

behaviour on that night was nothing to be ashamed of."

John Webster, prosecuting, said: "He objected when his friend was arrested for drunkenness and urinating against the wall of the club.

"He remonstrated with police and was abusive. This caused alarm to other people nearby."

Insp Stewart Hamilton of South Shields police said Sharpe swore at officers and "waved his arms wildly as we tried to get his friend into a police van.

"I was fearful that he might assault an officer and he was gesturing to other people who had gathered to watch."

But Philip Cordrey, defending, said there was no case to answer because no-one had witnessed the exchange between Sharpe and the two officers involved.

"There is no evidence to suggest that Mr Sharpe had caused any harassment, alarm, or distress to anyone.

"The police officers involved were certainly not alarmed by him and they have produced no-one else to support the view that he caused a disturbance to anyone else."

'Champ Cleared Over Police Clash' (news clipping, 1992)

ATHLETE DAVID IS 'ON THE RUN'

STAR athlete David Sharpe did a "runner" when he was due to appear in court on an assault charge following an alleged punch-up outside a pub.

The case had to be adjourned on Friday after magistrates were told he was representing Britain at an international athletics meeting in Turin, Italy.

It was the second time that Sharpe, 25, of Roman Road, Jarrow, Tyneside, had shown the court a clean pair of heels.

A fortnight earlier the hearing was cancelled while he competed in Zurich.

Defending solicitor Philip Cordery explained the situation to Hebburn magistrates on Tyneside.

The Crown Prosecution Service agreed to adjourn the case for another week until Sharpe, who is expected to plead not guilty, can appear.

But last night the Lord

PEOPLE REPORTER

Chancellor's office, which is in charge of magistrates' courts, denied he was given preferential treatment.

A spokesman said: "A decision is made by magistrates on the day for the reasons put forward."

● SHARPE finished last in the Grand Prix season final in Turin and missed out on the prize money.

DOG DEATH-ALERT

GRIEVING Alfie Barney, of Hindon, near Salisbury, discovered his wife Daisy was dead after their dog limped home alone. Both had been hit by a tractor.

Girl, 4 hunted

LITTLE Laura Konan, four, was being hunted by Interpol last night after her French father failed to return her to her mother Rosalyn Wigham's home in Blyth, Northumberland, after a day out.

'Athlete David is on the Run' (news clipping, 1992)

The Journal/Saturday, September 5, 1992

Experts still baffled by tanker fireball riddle

BAFFLED accident investigators still don't know why the Sunderland fireball petrol tanker caught fire so quickly in last week's crash.

Health and Safety Executive and Department of Transport officials have found marks along the tanker's sides.

But the investigators don't know whether the half-inch marks were there before last Wednesday's Newcastle Road accident.

Yesterday an HSE spokesman said: "We are still carrying out detailed investigations to find out how the faults came about."

The investigators are mystified as to why the three-year-old tanker broke up and caught fire so quickly

The HSE spokesman added: "We have found nothing which raises any suspicions about the condition of the vehicle and the driver was very experienced"

Police are still trying to trace a blue Ford Transit van, which the tanker driver said blocked his path seconds before the crash.

■ **Mystery fireball:** The blazing tanker in Newcastle Road, Sunderland.

RUNNER SHOWS COURT CLEAN PAIR OF HEELS — AGAIN

'Prize guy' wins more court time

INTERNATIONAL athlete David Sharpe has made a second false start in his head-to-head race with the law — running for prize money instead of appearing before a court.

The 800m runner showed Hebburn magistrates a clean pair of heels yesterday by running in last night's lucrative Turin final of the Grand Prix season.

It's the second time in three weeks Sharpe, 25, of Roman Road, Jarrow, has

By PAUL DUTTON

Zurich when he should have faced a charge of assault occasioning actual bodily harm at South Shields magistrates.

That hearing was adjourned until yesterday, but magistrates adjourned the case again for seven days after learning Sharpe had packed his bags and flown to Italy.

Last night the Lord Chancellor's office, responsible for overseeing magistrates' decisions, denied Sharpe was being given preferential treatment.

A spokesman said: "A decision is made by magistrates on the day for the reasons put forward."

Sharpe's solicitor, Philip Cordery, told the bench the runner was representing Britain in last night's race.

Dennis Scully, prosecuting, said the Crown Prosecution Service had no objection to the adjournment after they were telephoned with an explanation earlier this week.

> ▶ **Sharpe in Turin:** Page 55 ▶

> QUOTE
>
> ❝ A decision is made by magistrates on the day for the reasons put forward. ❞
>
> — LORD CHANCELLOR'S OFFICE

competed in prize money races instead of appearing before magistrates.

On August 19 he ran in

■ **David Sharpe:** Ran for prize money.

Garage hit by massive blaze

A £250,000 blaze has destroyed a garage and dozens of new cars.

The New City Cars garage on Waterville Road — on the edge of the Meadow Well Estate in North Shields — was gutted when a fireball ripped through the showroom and office complex.

Fifty new and used cars were burnt out as residents reported seeing flames as high as 40 feet engulf the Proton dealers on Thursday night.

But police and fire officers, who spent most of yesterday sifting through the remains, have ruled out arson.

Investigations into the cause are still continuing.

At the height of the blaze more than 40 firemen and 11 appliances from across Tyne and Wear were at the scene.

Firemen, who took more than two hours to extinguish the flames, were worried that sparks might set alight a garage on the opposite side of the road.

Tynemouth's acting station officer Bill Hadfield, said: "The whole place was absolutely devas-

'Prize Guy Wins More Court Time' (news clipping, 1992)

THE SHIELDS
Gazette

Monday, November 9, 1992   BRITAIN'S OLDEST PROVINCIAL EVENING NEWSPAPER   25p

'STAR HIT ME' CLAIM

Police hit by boozer ban

POLICE in Jarrow have been barred from their own boozer!

The social club at Jarrow Police Station in Clervaux Terrace has been shut down after its drinks licence was not renewed.

Chief Inspector Alan Nichol said the club had been closed for a few days "because of a clerical oversight."

He said: "Normally the licensing court sends out reminders to clubs in the area, telling them their licenses are due for renewal in three months' time, or whatever.

"But this practice has stopped and there was no application made. We believe this has affected one other club in the area. Now it is up to clubs to keep an eye out when their licences are due for renewal."

The club has been shut for almost a week, and could be closed for a number of weeks until the licence is approved by South Tyneside licensing justices.

Model Julie in Page 3 muddle

THE chance of instant modelling fame for South Shields beauty Julie Rogers has been put on ice after a national newspaper mix-up.

A glamour shot of the leggy teenager was due to appear in The Sun - giving millions of readers the opportunity to see her good looks.

But when 18-year-old Julie opened the popular tabloid, she found a complete stranger in her place.

She said: "I couldn't believe it. The phone hasn't stopped ringing from friends trying to find out what has happened.

"I wanted to be seen in a national newspaper to give my career a boost because it's my dream to break into modelling in a big way.

"I only hope The Sun can put the proper picture of me in the paper as soon as possible. It is my big ambition to appear on page 3."

A spokesman for The Sun confirmed there had been a mix-up with the photograph.

He said: "We can only apologise to Julie and hopefully get things right next time."

Julie, who works for the Boldon-based model agency LA Promotions, has been likened to a young Brigitte Bardot and is hoping to pursue an acting career.

MODEL MUDDLE ... for Julie Rogers.

BY PAUL KELLY

INTERNATIONAL athlete David Sharpe ran away from the police after allegedly attacking a Jarrow mechanic, a court was told.

David Pattison told Hebburn Magistrates Sharpe punched him in the face during a late night attack outside the Venue pub in South Shields on July 11 of this year.

Sharpe, who won the World Cup 800 metres championship race in Cuba in September, is alleged to have run away from the police in the direction of South Shields Market Place, where he was caught and detained.

Mr Pattison, of Lancaster Way, Jarrow, said the assault followed a skirmish inside the pub.

Argument

Mr Pattison's friend, Christopher Pratt, had an argument with Sharpe on the stairs of the pub, the court was told.

Mr Pattison said: "I heard someone say 'it's all your fault'. I thought to myself 'what have I done wrong'. I had never spoken to Mr Sharpe until I was hit."

Mr Pattison suffered a bust nose and fat lip from the alleged attack.

Sharpe 25, of Roman Road, Jarrow, pleaded not guilty to assault occasioning actual bodily harm.

Proceeding.

'STAR HIT ME claim' (news clipping, 1992)

Gazette SPORT

£100 PRIZE NUMBER

£100 WINNER J5782

Mansell claims pole spot

BELGIUM GRAND PRIX

NIGEL MANSELL is all set to claim his ninth success of a marvellous season at tomorrow's Belgian Grand Prix.

The newly-crowned Formula 1 king was confident provisional pole position and most also feel better after he was no longer interested in driving for Williams next year.

Mansell lapped the high-speed circuit in 1min 50.545secs at an average speed of 141.123 mph — more than two seconds faster than nearest rival Senna and three seconds ahead of his

Williams team-mate Riccardo Patrese.

Senna's decision leaves just Mansell, Patrese and Frenchman Alain Prost still scrapping for places.

And Mansell insisted that he was more motivated than ever after winning the championship and desperately wanted to clinch the constructors' title for Williams.

He declared: "I am more committed this before — not less. I want to grab that ninth win badly."

Botham injury doubt

COUNTY CRICKET

DURHAM will give their England all-rounder Ian Botham a fitness test today, but it is hoped that he will be able to play in tomorrow's Sunday League clash with Yorkshire at Darlington.

Skipper David Graveney is also expected to play despite splitting a finger on his left hand when fielding a ball against Hampshire yesterday.

Botham has seen a Harley Street specialist about his troublesome shoulder, and has had an injection to ease movement in the joint.

Meanwhile, Durham could well see

the last day of the match with Hampshire end in a washout as the forecast predicts heavy rains today.

However, they will be hoping the weather clears up in time for them to want to win their final Sunday League match of the season.

If the match goes ahead, Durham should be in with a chance against a Yorks side who have lost seven Sunday matches on the trot — but who have beaten Durham twice already this season.

NEWS IN BRIEF

Davies hunts third victory

BRITAIN's Laura Davies has two strokes to make up today as she hunts her third win of the season — in the IBM Open at Haninge near Stockholm.

Davies, with rounds of 68 and 72 lies third — two strokes adrift of Helen Alfredson, who started the day at eight under par on 138 and one shot clear of Annika Sorenstam, another Swede.

The former British and US Open champion, has bettered par in each of her last 10 rounds but slipped back with two expensive holes yesterday.

Tester for Cram

JARROW's World mile record holder Steve Cram certainly faces a stern test next month when he faces Spain's Olympic 1500 metres champion Fermin Cacho in the Standard Life Princes Street Mile in Edinburgh on September 13.

Wigan off to flyer

WIGAN boss John Monie is refusing to get carried away by the champions' flying start to the new campaign.

He watched them thrash first division newcomers Sheffield Eagles 46-5 last night to end their opening day as — they had not won their first League game for three seasons — but then issued a note of caution.

"I was happy to get the two points, but we've still got to measure up against the likes of St Helens and Leeds," warned the Australian coach.

He's a winner!

THE lucky-winner of our recent Sportspack Olympic competition is John Normansdale of Palm Avenue South Shields.

John wins a superb £30 pair of trainers provided by sponsor John pack of Sportspack - so b. shouldn't have any excuse for ducking out of training for next month's diet Coke Great North Run!

LATEST LATEST LATEST
NEWS DESK 4554661

HAPPY SHARPE PROVES POINT

DAVID SHARPE made a personal point last night - despite finishing third over 800 metres in last night's Memorial Van Damme IAAF/Mobil Grand Prix meeting.

The Jarrow athlete finished strongly ahead of the British contingent, only beaten by William Tanui and Nixon Kiprotich the Kenyans who took the Olympic gold and silver medals in Barcelona.

By DAVID MARTIN in Brussels

Tanui won in 1min 45.05sec, 0.20sec quicker than his colleague who Sharpe running 1min 42.25sec.

However, Sharpe once again defeated his two British arch-rivals European champion Tom McKean of Scotland who was sixth, and Liverpool's Curtis Robb who finished dead last!

It was another brilliant performance by the 25-year-old. Indeed the gap between him and the winner suggested that if he had been in Barcelona, a place in the final if not a medal, could well have been his.

"I'm happy with my run," he told me immediately following the race.

"It was a solid run and that's what I wanted."

And Sharpe, overlooked for the Great Britain's World Cup team in Havana next month might still be making the journey to Cuba. Robb selected on the strength of his seventh place in the Olympic final was the selectors' first choice.

Beaten

But last night the 20-year-old who is being hailed as heir apparent to Sebastian Coe, suggested he might withdraw. A knee injury has been troubling him and it seems he may have run his last race of the season.

This would leave the way clear for Sharpe who has beaten him in their last four clashes, to replace him.

Certainly after his 1min 43.98sec performance in Zurich last week, the South Tyneside must be the obvious choice.

In the race Sharpe was last at the bell, and nearly 15 metres down on the pacemaker Lukas Sang who paced in in 49.91sec.

It might be argued the European silver-medallist left things a little late, but he was more than happy with his 57.4sec first lap, and quickly moved through the field along the back straight.

Running 26.7sec for the final 200 metres, Sharpe was the fastest finisher, but couldn't quite break the Kenyans.

Sharpe said: "Running 1min 45sec here seems so easy. I probably concentrated to much on beating McKean and Robb and if I had decided to take on Tanui earlier, I might have got him, I was finishing like a train."

Colin Walker of Gateshead Harriers was a creditable sixth in the steeplechase when the Kenyans led by Philip Barkutwo who won in 8min 12.70sec took the first three places.

Slower

The Frankland prison officer recorded 8min 25.49sec run, 0.34sec slower than his personal best.

Linford Christie has been beaten by only one man this year, Olapade Adeniken. And the Nigerian who is rapidly becoming a bogeyman to Briton's Olympic champion, inflicted his fourth defeat on Christie winning by 0.03sec in 10.12sec.

Shilton has no complaints

FORMER England goalkeeper Peter Shilton said that he had no complaints about being sent off last night - for the first time in his 29-year career.

The Plymouth player-manager, who a record England 125 caps, received his marching orders as his side lost a division two match 2-0 at Hull last night.

"We abide by the referee's decisions at Plymouth. Referees make mistakes — although I am not saying that this was one."

Shilton was sent-off in the 36th minute after a mix-up let in Hull's Graeme Atkinson, who was set to score.

Last night's football

BARCLAYS LEAGUE
Division One
Tranmere 2 2-1 Bristol Rov
Division Two
Hull City 2-0 Plymouth A
Division Three
Crewe Alex 3-2 Northampton

IMPRESSIVE PERFORMANCE ... from David Sharpe as he led the Brits home.

INSIDE: Teams, Cricket - P22; Sunday Football, Fishing - P22; Darts P23.

Published by Northeast Press Limited, Chapter Row, South Shields, NE33 1BL. (Tel: 061 4554661) and printed by them at Sunderland. Registered as a newspaper at the Post Office. All advertisements within the Gazette are publisher's copyright and may not be reproduced in any form without written permission. Saturday, August 29th, 1992

'Happy Sharpe Proves Point' (news clipping, Ivo Van Damme, 1992)

GOLDEN BOY: David Sharpe produced an electric finish to win World 800m gold medal

LOOKING SHARPE

DAVID Sharpe ran the race of his life today.

The Jarrow runner stormed home to win the 800m for Great Britain in the World Cup in Havana, Cuba.

He joined with Linford Christie, who won the 100m, and Jon Ridgeon, second in the 400m hurdles, to give Great Britain an unexpected lead after the first day's competition.

Sharpe produced one of his typical express finishes to take the gold medal.

The 25-year-old ghosted through from seventh at the bell, squeezed past two Olympic finalists Andrea Benvenuti and Jose-Luis Barbosa on the home straight and then pipped Olympic champion William Tanui in the final few strides to win in 1min 46.06secs.

BEST

"I've got to the point where I now know I can beat the best in the world and that they are worried about me," said Steve Cram's pal, who reckons the win has given him confidence that he can win a

Jarrow star grabs World 800m gold

world championship medal in Stuttgart next year.

Christie proved beyond doubt that he is the greatest 100 metres sprinter in the world.

Following his emphatic defence of the World Cup 100 metres crown and his destruction of Olapade Adeniken, the only man to have beaten him over the distance this term, Olympic champion Christie said: "I don't see how they can't say I'm the world's No.1 now."

Christie demonstrated his supremacy in familiar style, ignoring the treacherous conditions on a rain-sodden track to jet away from the blocks first and power home in 10.21secs, two strides clear of Adeniken (10.26), with American veteran Calvin Smith third.

"I've run about 30-odd races this year and to lose just four altogether isn't a bad record," said Christie. "But, more to the point, I've won all the important ones."

He now plans to become the first man to achieve a golden sprint double in the World Cup when he goes in the 200 metres tomorrow.

Ridgeon's silver in the one-lap hurdles was even more of a surprise and he was agonisingly close to earning a sensational victory over Zambia's world champion Samuel Matete when he led off the last hurdle.

Only one of the African's famed late surges saw him inch ahead at the tape. 48.88secs to 49.01secs.

Spurs bid to halt Waddle

CHRIS Waddle returns to White Hart Lane tomorrow with his former Tottenham team-mates on full alert to stop him stealing the show.

Waddle moved to top French side Marseilles for £4.25m in 1989 before returning to England and Sheffield Wednesday for £1m this summer.

He is set to face his old club in front of BSkyB's cameras and Tottenham coach knows Waddle would love to impress.

Livermore said today:"Chris Waddle is a world class player and no-one knows that better than we do.

"He was a great player for us here at Tottenham and I'm sure he would like to put one over on us tomorrow — we must make sure that he doesn't."

Wednesday's defender turned striker Paul Warhurst will also be a centre of attention.

He's set to return to action just 11 days following his brush with death after swallowing his tongue when knocked unconscious in the UEFA Cup tie against Spora Luxembourg.

Warhurst, who celebrates his 23rd birthday today, has come through his first light training session without ill effect and yesterday joined in a full work out with the Wednesday squad.

Also in the spotlight will be young Tottenham striker Nicky Barmby who looks set to make his debut in the absence of £2.2m striker Gordon Durie.

Gazza on way back

PAUL Gascoigne will tomorrow play his first meaningful 45 minutes of soccer since the 1991 FA Cup final.

Gascoigne will end over 16 months of pain, fear and frustration when, as expected, he steps out in Rome's Olympic Stadium in a Lazio shirt to face Genoa.

Lazio coach Dino Zoff is expected to formally announce his team within the next 24 hours and Gazza can expect to be in the starting line-up for the first time since his £5.5 million move from Tottenham.

'Looking Sharpe' (news clipping, World Cup)

'Golden Boy Sharpe' (news clipping, World Cup)

'Top of the World' (news clipping, World Cup)

Chapter Twelve

Cancer

Jarrow, the 2000s

WHEN I was growing up, we must have had one of the smallest families in the area. Up until my brother and his partner had their son, Lewis, there were only five of us. My mam, dad, brother and nanna and I all lived in the same house. I had no aunties, uncles or cousins. It was great at Christmas time because we didn't have a lot of presents to buy.

We were exceptionally close, especially me and my mam. We had similar personalities. Mam was renowned for being kind. She'd rather give than receive. I remember when I was a kid going on holiday to the Lake District on my parents' wedding anniversary, Mam had planned to buy Dad a ring. But he said he wasn't bothered, so instead of buying him a ring, Mam bought us a rubber dinghy. So, because our dad wasn't bothered about a ring, me and my brother got something to play with instead. That was typical of our mam.

Mam used to sell raffle tickets for the local hospice. First prize was a hamper. I can remember very clearly coming home from work one day and Mam said to me, 'Right, don't ask any questions, go and take that empty hamper and this 40 quid down to the shops and fill the hamper up with food.'

And I went, 'What for?'

'I told you, don't ask questions, I just want you to go.'

So I went down the shops and when I got back with a full hamper, Mam said, 'I want you to go and deliver it to this address.'

Now I didn't know that she'd been out earlier in the day and knocked on the door at that address to sell raffle tickets, or that when the woman answered the door, Mam noticed a few kids running about barefoot and that there were no carpets. The woman had said she didn't have much money so she'd just buy one ticket, not a strip. But Mam said, 'It's all right, I'll put it in for you.'

Because Mam had noticed that they didn't have a lot, she decided that she'd pretend that the woman had won first prize. And that's when I delivered the hamper, even though it was three or four days before the draw had even been made. Mam had used her own money for me to fill up the hamper.

CANCER

On the other hand, Mam also had a fierce temper. That's how she and I were most alike. I'd also rather give than receive, and I've got a fierce temper as well. It must have been the ginger hair. I don't know how else to explain it but me and me mam had a special type of bond. Even after I moved out of the house, I'd still see her almost every day.

Mam died of cancer in 2004. Long before that, she'd been diagnosed with diabetes when she was in her 50s, and had to take pills. She was on insulin ten years later. I'd sometimes measure her blood sugar for her. Mam would be sitting there saying, 'Come on, hurry up, you're taking too long. I know it's going to be too high.'

'Mam, what do you mean: you know it's going to be too high?'

'Because it always is.'

And sure enough it was. I said to Dad that I didn't know what to do. Then when I went to the linen cupboard to get a towel, a packet of chocolate eclairs fell out.

'Mam, what's this?'

'I've only had one or two and I'm not giving up things that I like.'

Mam loved her sweets, but I said, 'One or two is too many, it's all sugar. It's enough to set your blood sugar levels too high.'

135

'I'm not bliddy bothered. If that's the way it goes, that's just the way it goes.'

My nanna went on like that too. She had heart disease, angina and diabetes. Both of them, throughout the last 20 years or so of their lives, never ever stopped eating what they enjoyed. They had sweets and chocolate hidden all ower the house. For two people to have the illnesses that they had and still go on and say, 'I'm not giving up what I enjoy,' and for Mam to live to 78 and Nanna to 91 without changing anything – when a lot of other people would just cut down on sugar and try to eat healthily – doesn't really make sense. They were both set in their ways.

I can remember coming home from clubbing with Whitey at about half two in the morning. When we pulled up in a taxi, Whitey noticed that all the lights were on in our house. I explained that this wasn't unusual; it would be my mam or nan up 'pouching'. As it happened, both of them were in the sitting room chatting and having a cup of tea. My nanna with an apple slice in her hand and my mam with a piece of sponge cake. It was the middle of the night and Whitey was finding it hilarious. He'd tell the story many times over.

Mam had the cancer for three or four weeks, then went into hospital and they couldn't operate, so they had her on morphine. I'm not saying I prepared myself but I knew that she was dying. It was so quick, which most people say is a good thing. But it's always devastating to lose a parent.

* * *

A year after Mam died, I had a pain in my groin and went to the doctor, who said that it was an infection in my testicle. I took antibiotics to clear up the infection and had a scan to find out what else might be going on. The surgeon got a pen and notepad and drew a circle about the size and shape of a testicle, and inside he put five dots. He said it was a build-up of calcium, which meant that I was susceptible to testicular cancer. They were going to give me ultrasound and take blood tests twice a year for the next five years.

The infection was soon gone, and the tests after the first six months were no problem. After a year, still no problem. And that went on for five years.

When the five years were nearly up, I happened to be looking at my bank statement and noticed that there was £28 coming out every month. I didn't know what it was for. I thought it was something to do with my mortgage, maybe a box I'd ticked or whatever. So I rang the bank I'd arranged my mortgage through, and I asked them what it was for. They said it was mortgage protection insurance. I asked if I needed to pay it, if it was the law. They said no but if anything ever happened to me, like if had a life-threatening condition that caused me to lose my job and couldn't ever work again, my mortgage would be paid for me. I told her that I was paying my mortgage but I didn't want this extra £28 a month taken out, and if I couldn't ever work again, I'd go and live with my dad. So she cancelled it.

And what should happen only a few weeks later? It was the last time in the five years that the hospital wanted me in for the six-monthly tests, and they found a lump in my testicle. I was diagnosed with testicular cancer, a life-threatening condition. Had I not cancelled the insurance I'd have had my mortgage paid off. Had my cancer come a bit earlier, before I spotted the insurance payment and cancelled it – but that's beside the point.

The surgeon said they didn't know whether the lump was malignant or benign but they couldn't take a risk. I asked the surgeon what he thought I should do. He said he couldn't advise me but if it was his son, he'd say to have the testicle removed. However, he told me that they'd taken someone's out the other month and there was nowt wrong with it. I said that, well, I'd have it done anyway.

Going in for the operation, I can remember the anaesthetist saying that my heart rate was too low for someone who should be anxious about going into surgery. He asked me if I did a lot of exercise, and I said aye, I used to, and I wasn't anxious.

I was in on a Monday and out on a Friday. This happened when I was working for the council. My boss had been on his holidays and when he came back I told him I had only one bollock left. He was like, 'What d'ye mean?'

'Well, since you've been away I've been diagnosed with cancer, had a bollock cut off and now the cancer's gone.'

I still had a blasé outlook on life, and the cancer was no different. I had two sessions of chemotherapy, and that was it. Honestly, it was like water off a duck's back. I don't know if that's a good thing or a bad thing because cancer, to certain people, is like a bolt of lightning out of the sky that knocks them for six. Maybe I should have been a lot more worried than I was, but it didn't faze me one little bit. I didn't attach too much importance to how serious it could have been if the cancer hadn't been caught so early. If the surgeon had said it had spread further, I'd probably have had a different attitude.

I suppose what I'm trying to say is – my shin splints when I was running, not getting the insurance money and even having testicular cancer – a life-threatening condition – it's no big thing compared with what some people have to go through.

* * *

My dad never had anything wrong with him until nine months before he died, in 2016. He had a tumour in his small intestine. He had it for eight or nine months without telling me anything. He was blending his food because of problems with his digestion. He told me he was going into hospital and he wanted me to drop him off. I was like, 'What do you mean, drop you off. Can you not take your car?'

The day before he went into hospital he was washing his car like he was fit as a fiddle. I had absolutely no inclination that there was anything wrong with him. But all that time, he knew he had a tumour and kept it quiet. When he asked me to drop him off at hospital I had no idea whatsoever that he wouldn't be coming back out.

Then I found a couple of letters from the hospital saying that the last resort was a stent to try to bypass this large tumour. And failing that, it was more than likely going to be a case of palliative care.

So I went into hospital and asked Dad, 'What the hell's this? What you been hiding your letters for? Why have you never told me?'

He said, 'It was something you didn't need to know.'

I don't know whether that was right or wrong but if I'd have known eight months earlier, that would have been eight months of me worrying about how much longer he had to live. So from his point of view it was probably a good idea.

One of the times me and Silke went to see him in hospital, I'd broken my glasses and I asked him to lend me his. Dad said, 'Wait until next week and you can keep them.'

I've often spoken to Silke about it, how he knew he wasn't coming out of hospital, that he hadn't long to live, and could still make a joke about it. I hope that when my time comes, I'll have that type of humour.

* * *

I can honestly say that I think about Jimmy all the time. Jimmy had heart problems. When he was 56, before I met him, he was out running and didn't feel well. Later, in hospital, he was told he'd had a heart attack. His wife, Connie, asked, 'Jim, do you know what day it is?'

And Jimmy was like, 'It's Saturday.'

Connie said, 'It's the same date that your dad died of a heart attack and you're the same age as he was.'

Jimmy had to have a coronary bypass. Later, when he was coaching me, he'd show me his scars and say, 'Feel this!' I think in those days the surgeons had to break ribs to do a bypass.

He told me that he'd asked the surgeon, 'How long does this bypass last, me bonny lad?' and the surgeon

141

told him ten years. So when the ten years were up, Jimmy went right back to the hospital to see what the deal was. Apparently he told the surgeon, 'Right, I've had my ten years. I could pop my clogs tomorrow, so I want testing so I can get a new bypass.'

And supposedly the surgeon replied, 'When I told you ten years ago that the bypass would last ten years, I didn't mean that in ten years' time you could come back asking for another one.'

Apart from getting a bit short of breath, nothing had triggered Jimmy to get checked out again other than it had been ten years since the last bypass. But remember that Jimmy had a magic wand. He wangled it, got tested and he did have another bypass, a triple one this time.

Since Jimmy died, I keep remembering story after story after story.

There was the time we decided to go to see the film *Misery* (from the Stephen King book) when we were away at an athletics event in 1990. We got our popcorn and drinks and sat down in front of two couples. Jimmy was hard of hearing, so whenever he spoke it was usually a bit loud. In the film, a writer, played by James Caan, crashes his car and injures himself. Kathy Bates's character, his number one fan, rescues him and then keeps him prisoner in her remote house. We'd got to the bit when Kathy Bates goes out shopping and

James Caan, who can't walk, drags himself out of the bedroom to try to phone for help. However, the phone isn't working, then he hears her coming back and, in his rush to get back to the room, he knocks this little toy penguin off the table. He stops to put the penguin back, so that she doesn't know he was trying to escape, but he faces it the wrong way.

Jimmy nudged me in the arm and said loudly, 'The silly booger. You know what's gonna to happen here, don't you? He's put the bliddy penguin back the wrong way. Ooh, he's in big trouble now.'

Unbeknown to Jimmy, I'd seen the film before, so I knew what was coming next. I started laughing and so did the two couples behind us, but Jimmy carried on unawares.

'Oh, you know what's happening now, don't you? She's gonna find out.'

Of course Jimmy was right: when Kathy Bates comes back the first thing she notices is the penguin facing the wrong way.

'What did I tell you?' asked Jimmy, nudging me again. 'The stupid booger's put the penguin back the wrong way.'

Me and the two couples were nearly peeing ourselves laughing. Meanwhile, Kathy Bates gets this big block of wood and ties it between James Caan's ankles. Then she fetches a big mallet – 'Bliddy big trouble now,' said Jimmy. 'She's got a mallet.' She smashes his ankle. 'Well, there you go,' said Jimmy. 'Serves the bliddy fool right. If he'd been driving his car properly he wouldn't have come off the bliddy road, silly booger. That's the moral of the story.'

By this time me and the two couples were in hysterics, while Jimmy went on and on: 'That'll happen to you one day, Sharpey, the way you drive. I keep telling you to slow down. Look what's happened to him.'

Nevertheless, Jimmy trusted me to drive his three-wheeler car once. We were going to a sportsman's dinner in Newcastle. I'd said to Jimmy that I'd pick him up in my car, but when I turned the key the battery was flat. When I phoned Jimmy to explain he said, 'Well, what do you want me to do about it?'

'We'll have to go in your car,' I said.

Jimmy was worried about being late, so I said I'd drive. As a big fan of motorsports, I'd been lucky enough to drive some fast cars. Driving Jimmy's three-wheeler was absolutely horrendous. It was all different shades of green on the outside because every time Jimmy had to patch up the paintwork he could never match the colour. Inside it was so cramped that my head was bumping against the roof, my knees could hardly fit in and my feet were getting stuck between the pedals because they were too close together. It was a nightmare to drive. When we got to 40mph on the Tyne Bridge, the gearstick slipped out of fourth and into neutral. I asked Jimmy what was going on with his car and what I should do about the gears.

'Just slip it back in,' he said. 'You're going too fast. I keep telling you about your driving.'

Anyway, we eventually reached Newcastle Civic Centre car park. Now, as you know, no matter how fast or slow you drive in an underground car park, when you take the corners the tyres screech like you're in a car chase.

'Slow down!' Jimmy was shouting as I pulled into a space and parked his tiny, patched-up three-wheeler next to a huge, immaculate Rolls-Royce. Who should be getting out of it but Sir John Hall, owner of Newcastle United FC. Sir John Hall looked at Jimmy, and Jimmy, who was black and white through and through, looked at Sir John Hall and said, 'What the bliddy hell's happening with our team?'

'What do you mean, Jimmy?' asked Sir John.

'What you need, me bonny lad,' answered Jimmy, 'is someone with a bit of leg speed down the wing. Sharpey would be your man – obviously he's quick enough – but he cannot kick a ball to save himself, so that's out of the question.'

'Okay, Jimmy,' said Sir John. 'We'll talk about it when we get inside.'

I found this hilarious, but that was Jimmy: straight to the point.

* * *

Things that happen in daily life now, every time I pass Mam and Dad's house, I think about them both. The other day I was looking at the only photograph I have of me and my nanna, and I remembered when she came out of the bathroom with a big towel tied round her head and tucked underneath her hair.

Dropping flowers off at Connie's house round about Christmas time, thinking about the times I spent with Jimmy, all the trips to race abroad, his coaching, the advice and the help he always gave me, his cats, flip-flops and three-wheeler car.

* * *

I'm a great believer that when a parent or close friend dies it's easier to accept if they've lived to a ripe old age. It was heartbreaking when they died, but I can't help thinking about other families who have much worse to deal with.

I met a young lad of 17 on the cancer ward. He and a much older guy were having their chemo at the same time as me. The older guy was a golfer and the young lad had been on about taking up golf. So when the older guy finished his chemo, he came back with some golf magazines for the young lad, but the nurse had to tell him that he'd passed away.

Stories like that, when you look at my parents, my nanna and Jimmy, who lived good lives and had children, and you think about this young kid who hadn't even reached 18, you sort of accept what happened to your family. Whether or not other people compare things like that the way I do, I don't know, but it makes it easier for me to deal with the hurt of losing someone close. Imagine what this young lad's parents must have been going through.

Chapter Thirteen
Taken Too Soon

Jarrow, the 2000s

TO ME, a life-threatening condition doesn't necessarily mean cancer or heart disease. It's also mental illness. Two people I was really close to took their own lives. My best mate, Whitey, and Silke's middle son, Julian. Both of them were taken far too soon.

Whitey committed suicide on an oil rig. I didn't even know that he was suffering really bad with mental health problems.

A couple of days before he went on the rig he seemed right as rain. I don't suppose it's a spur of the moment thing to take your own life. People killed in an accident don't have a choice but with suicide they must think about it long and hard. But Whitey was happy before he left to go on the oil rig. Or so we thought, which I find really sad.

He went down to the lowest part of the rig, just above the surface of the sea, and hung himself. When I heard about that I realised that we hadn't been as close as we used to be. I thought about when we were closer, and I felt guilty. I wondered, if we'd still spoken a bit more or knocked about with each other as much as we used to, would it have been the same outcome? Then I started thinking about when we had the odd disagreement. There was a lot of other things going on in his life but if I'd been a bigger part of his life towards the end, would it have helped?

It was so similar with Silke's middle son, Julian. When I first met him, he was 13. He left to go and live with his dad in America when he was 16. That was February or March and he committed suicide that May. Putting the two together, I think about the couple of arguments we had and wonder whether it made any difference. I knew Whitey from when we were nine or ten and Julian for three or four years, and sometimes I forget about all the good times and wonder about the few times that we had an argument. I think that's human nature.

But we shouldn't dwell on what might have been. It's a bit like someone letting their bairn go to the shop on their pushbike and the bairn gets knocked over. The parent thinks they should never have let them go to the shop anyway. How do you deal with it? We've got to think of the people who are still alive, and accept that if someone decides to take their own life, whatever's going on in their mind, they don't think about the consequences. We need to accept that we're still alive and have to try to understand why they've done it. I'm a great believer that if someone is at the end of their tether, we've got to sympathise and empathise, rather than say what some people think, which is that suicide is an easy way out or a coward's way out. I don't go down that road one little bit. I've never been in that situation but I tend to think that there's not enough support out there for people who are still alive to deal with what's happened.

* * *

Whitey and I went to the same school and lived around the corner from each other. I lived on Roman Road and he lived in Langley Terrace in Primrose, Jarrow, where we grew up. Whitey was a well-liked character. A lot of people knew him as 'Smiler'. He had a unique outlook on life, and the clothes he used to wear and the things he'd do were unique too. My mam was very fond of Whitey and I remember one time he knocked for me on a Friday night after he'd been up to Newcastle shopping. I was upstairs getting ready and I heard my mam saying to him, 'What the bliddy hell you got on?' He had this new cowhide jacket, all black with little bits of white on. 'And what have you got on your face?'

He'd put this false tan on, and I went, 'Whitey, what's gang on? Your face is covered in brown.'

And Whitey turned to my mam and said, 'Do you know how it is, Mary? I'm just trying to look my best. All me and David are going out for is the lasses.'

Unlike me, Whitey was a good-looking kid. He had a full head of spiky black hair, whereas I had ginger all ower. He always got tapped up by lasses but I had to work for it.

Whitey was always in trouble with the law. Not anything major, always petty stuff. Not a bad lad.

Once I bought this jeep off him. He'd got it for £5,000 or £6,000 on a payment plan with a local garage, and after a couple of months he decided to sell it. I think I gave him £2,500 for it. Lo and behold, five or six months later, at about eight in the morning, *bang-bang-bang* on the door. It was the police with a big low-loader outside. 'We've come to take the jeep because the guy who bought it hasn't even paid the first month's instalment to the finance company.' They didn't say who it was or ask me if I knew him. The jeep got taken away all the same, which was embarrassing because the police had to block the whole street and hold up the traffic so they could get the jeep on the low-loader.

I went to see a local solicitor. (I told him a load of lies, like.) He said if you bought the jeep in good faith, then it's yours. (But I didn't buy it in good faith. I bought it because it was cheap. I knew it wasn't paid for.) The jeep stood for a year in the police compound and then I went to court in Newcastle. The finance company said, 'What we're proposing, Mr Sharpe, is that you bought the jeep knowing that it hadn't been paid for and you paid £2,500 pounds for a £5,000 or £6,000 jeep, which is way too cheap. We believe that it should go back to us.' But somehow I got the jeep back. It's not a great moral story, like.

One night at a derelict church in South Shields, even the coppers couldn't stop pissing themselves laughing at Whitey. He was pinching slates off the roof with three or four other lads. A copper came into the church shining his torch up. Whitey and two others were hiding in the spire. The coppers said, 'Look, we know you're up there and that something's going on. You'd better come down.'

The lads kept quiet for an hour or so, and then they came down and filled their transit van with thousands of slates. What the hell they were going to do with them all at four in the morning, I don't know. The van was pulled up going down York Avenue, which was the street next to where me and Whitey lived. The copper asked where they'd been and where they were going.

The driver said they were going to work as scaffolders. So the police opened the back door of the van and there was Whitey, black as the ace of spades, covered in dust off all these slates.

The copper just burst out laughing, saying, 'So you're on your way to work, are you? You're the ones that've been nicking slates.'

Whitey got done for that as well as the jeep fraud. He got three months in an open jail. One day he asked me to bring a crate of lager and 40 fags. 'I want you to pull up by the jail,' he said, 'and put the lager and fags behind the green electrical junction box right next to a small roundabout just outside the prison fence.' So I did. I didn't know what they were allowed or not allowed, or else I wouldn't have put them where I put them.

I don't think Whitey had much left of his sentence, but I got a phone call from him the following week and he said, 'See where you left me the lager and fags? I'm going to be there at six o'clock on Saturday and I'm coming back with you for a night out.'

And I went, 'Naw, that ain't gonna happen.'

But it did happen because his brother went to pick him up, which I discovered when I was out in a bar in South Shields at eight o'clock that same Saturday night.

Whitey came bowling in. 'Wey-hey, Sharpey! How you doin'?'

And I'm like, 'Whitey, what you doin'?'

'Ah, bollocks to them!'

He spent the evening in South Shields with me, got a curry on the way home to his house and then the police arrived at about one o'clock in the morning. He told me later that he hadn't even started his curry. He must have assumed the police didn't know what he looked like, so when they went, 'Right, Michael White,' he said, 'Na, na, not me, you've got the wrong person, my name's not Michael, piss off.'

'What's that on your arm, then?' (It was a tattoo with his name, Michael.) *Boosh*, lifted, banged up again, with an extra couple of months on to his sentence.

That was typical of Whitey. He was always go-happy, always smiling, laughing and carrying on. Whatever was going on within him to make him take his own life, he hid completely. None of us knew.

Which was exactly like Julian. He'd come home from school laughing and carrying on with his tie round his head. Always smiling and full of life. With mental illness and suicide you'll never ever know what people are hiding. Personality-wise, I'd put myself in the same category as them, although I've never thought of taking my own life. But if I'm feeling a bit down, I'll never admit it, I'll always hide it. What people see of me is the same as we saw of Whitey and Julian: all laughs and happiness. But the thought of people going through that mental illness for large parts of their lives, and us not knowing anything about it, is absolutely horrendous.

I got on well with Julian. When Silke came over here from Texas, Julian spent the rest of his childhood here in Hebburn. He went to the same secondary school as I did.

When he went to Texas to live with his dad, the lifestyle that his dad provided for him over there was a helluva lot better than we had. They had a big five-bedroomed bungalow in a cul-de-sac, double driveway, double garage, sprinklers going on the lawn. Whatever he was going through, we didn't know and couldn't work out why he'd done it. We still don't know. The funeral was awful.

Suicide is a terrible thing. When you have people close to you, it's hard to explain. I've spoken to Silke and Julian's friends and family over there, and the only way we'll ever know how people would want to do it is if we were in that situation. It's hard to try and work out the reasons. You can talk for days or weeks or months or years about why and how people want to do it and follow through with it, but we'll never ever know why. It's a hard one to come by.

The son of our neighbour's sister took his own life a year ago. What's helping Silke is that the sister started a local support group about mental illness. Silke goes once a month and it gives her the chance to talk about what happened in her case. I think it helps.

* * *

When I had cancer, it was gone quickly and I've been assured that it's 99 per cent certain that it won't come back. That was relatively easy to deal with. It was here and then it was gone. But mental ill health stays with you for much longer, sometimes years and years and years. You can't really comment on it unless you've been there yourself. And I haven't.

I've had ups and downs, like, but I've never had to take antidepressants or anything like that. There was a time when I worked for the council when I was down in the dumps. I was off sick for three months and I dealt with it. I remember hinting to the doctor that I might need a pill, but he more or less chased me.

Mental health is a big thing, especially with blokes. They don't want to talk about it, although I think that's getting better now.

A changing point about men's mental health for me was a few years ago when Prince Harry talked about what he went through as a kid when his mam died (not to be confused with his recent revelations and his 2023 book). He was sharing what he hadn't talked about before. I think that a lot of men might have said, 'Do you know what, if he can talk about it, so can I.'

I think, deep down, men still have a problem talking about mental health. I'm sure, even now it's a very small percentage of men with mental health problems that actually talk about them. Even if it's as high as 20 per cent who want to share what they're going through, that's 80 per cent who are not saying anything. I don't suppose we'll ever get to know how many of them there are and what it is they're not saying.

Silke thinks about Julian every day. In the early days after Julian died, she took an overdose and was in hospital for four days. Some people say that when people do that it's a cry for help. I don't think that's true. Not one little bit. I don't know how many people die after taking an overdose but it certainly can happen. If I hadn't found Silke when I did, it could have killed her.

It wasn't a cry for help. It was because Silke wanted to be with her son. I can understand why she wanted to do it. Some people who lose a loved one because of suicide go on to try to do it themselves.

I don't know whether we dealt with Julian's death well or badly. There's no right or wrong way about how somebody who has lost a child deals with it or how their partner deals with it. It differs so much from one parent or family to another. There's no rulebook.

I don't know whether time is a great healer or not. Julian's death changed Silke's life forever. For the worse. But I know that, as time goes on, Silke can deal with her loss better. She certainly hasn't healed, by a long way, and she never will. Things might get easier, but nothing's healed. Sometimes people suffer ten or 12 years later like it's just happened. When Julian died, time stood still for Silke. Run-of-the-mill stuff like shopping and chores about the house stopped for a while. She said that she didn't care about them any more.

Silke has moved on, without a doubt. But not a day goes by that she doesn't think about Julian.

Chapter Fourteen

Looking Back

Jarrow, present day

IF ANYONE had told me when I was 25 how I'd feel now at 55, I wouldn't have believed them. I'm knackered all the time. I'm convinced that my aches and pains are due to the high-intensity training that I used to do. After all, I don't think our bodies were made to cope with the stress that we put them through. Hence all the injuries.

I always had a problem with my shins when I was running. Now I've got a different pain in my lower leg. I think it's called peroneal tendonitis, which is new to me, and I'm not even running any more.

When I left my job with the council in 2016, I did something I'd always wanted to do and passed my HGV Class 2 licence. At the time of writing I'm on a Class 1 course. As a lorry driver I love travelling all over the country on the open road. I'm loading and unloading heavy stuff, which is physically demanding and keeps me fit. I also walk miles and miles in the countryside when I'm out birdwatching.

However, my back's painful too. God knows what I'll be like when I'm 65 or 75. It's just what you've got to deal with though, isn't it?

* * *

Back in the day when I was running races, looking back was something that I rarely did. But that's exactly what I'm going to do now.

I can remember funny stories about motorbikes, cars, charity boxing, skiing, birdwatching and getting into scrapes like it was yesterday but, when it comes to athletics details, I cannot remember a bliddy thing.

All the same, almost everything that I'm proud of is athletics-related, even though my career lasted only ten years or so. I'm absolutely over the moon with my achievements, the times I ran and the races I won. I found out recently that some of my junior records – which were set over 35 years ago – still stand today. Others were broken only in the past year or two. I was a young kid from a humble background in Jarrow who became World Junior champion, European Indoor champion and silver medallist outdoors, World Cup winner, and ran 1:43. You'd be mad not to be proud of all that. Had someone said to me when I was 16 or 17 that I was going to go on to achieve all that, I'd have been 100 per cent happy with it.

I'm certainly not proud of some of the things I've done that are not related to athletics. The way I used to ride motorbikes and drive cars, two or three run-ins with the law, frequenting houses of ill repute once or twice.

What's weird is, what I'm also proud of is being a good person. Especially since I've calmed down a lot.

Athletics put me on the road to learning the values of life and positive morals. I've often wondered whether, without athletics, I might have gone down a different road. When you get into a routine of training hard towards a goal, it makes you disciplined. I'm almost sure that if from an early age you can get yourself to the same place for training on the same day of the week and at the same time, week in, week out, you'll learn a lot about yourself. I'm sure athletics has made me a better person.

You could compare being an athlete with joining the army – something in life that you learn a lot from. I've met ex-forces personnel who've finished their service as better people. They're better organised, always on time, more polite and respectful. You'll always hear them saying something like: 'I was born here but I was made in the army.' It's like that with me too. I was born in Jarrow, but athletics made me.

* * *

I was never over-bothered about not going to the Olympic Games. I was disappointed at the time but it was short-lived because I didn't breathe, eat and sleep athletics like some other athletes did. Maybe my blasé attitude was the right one to have.

Some people reading this might beg to differ. They might say that I wasn't hungry enough for the Olympics. Some say that I was a wasted talent. They look at what I didn't do rather than what I did do. But if you put on one side of the scales all that I did achieve, and on the other side what I could or should have achieved, my actual achievements outweigh the rest.

But these people will put all that aside and *still* focus on what might have been. Maybe they haven't achieved much in their own lives, I don't know. I sort of get where they're coming from, but I'm not too sure. If you had a crystal ball you would be sure, but nobody has a crystal ball, do they? I *might* have gone on to get an Olympic medal but we'll never ever know.

It was never my only golden ambition to go to the Olympic Games, although some people think that athletics *is* the Olympics and nothing else matters. What they don't realise when they're criticising athletes is that those athletes are giving the best they can, and sometimes it isn't good enough. It doesn't make them a bad person. Someone sitting in an armchair doesn't see that.

In the era when I was competing, we had five or six men who could run 1:44. If you've got a group of athletes from the same country running so well, and all in the same race – well, I could finish anywhere from first to fifth. If I won – great. But if I tried my hardest, ran a really fast time and finished fourth or fifth – also great. I was nearly always quite happy within myself.

I trained my bollocks off but I didn't train as often as I should have done. What I lacked, apart from not training often enough, was the mental ability to become a better athlete. Sometimes I think that my talent was 90 per cent physical and natural but only ten per cent mental. If they'd been more evenly matched, god knows how quickly I'd have run or if I'd have gone to the Olympics. Friends tell me that I shouldn't put myself down as being daft but, if the truth be known and if I had one wish, it would be to have more mental ability. I wish I'd been more switched on about what it takes to become an Olympic champion. I never did well at school. I always struggled academically and I still do. I'm streetwise, I've got a load of common sense, I've learned things and become better at things, but I cannot change the way I was born. I've heard of top sportsmen who've written down when they were a kid that they were going to be the best in the world – and they were. But I never had the mental ability to do that or think that.

I had a good year, bad year, good year, bad year. Maybe the year after a good year I lived the life of Riley and did things I shouldn't have done and that's why I had a bad year. Did I take my eye off the ball?

* * *

I came across a comment on an athletics forum by accident recently. It was about athletes and drugs, which I've never been interested in. That forum discussion just goes to show what some of the general public think about what athletes might have been taking. You never knew who was and who wasn't. It's a sore subject. This one guy was going on about Crammy, Coe, Ovett and me. I was absolutely gobsmacked. I came in and showed Silke, and went, 'Can you believe this?'

I can't remember ever putting on any weight – I never used to do weight training – and as far as I'm concerned my weight was always about ten and a half stone when I was running, and my shoulders and arms were always the same size. But this guy spurted out that I must have taken something between 1991 and 1992 because all of a sudden I'd got much bigger and ran a lot faster. Which is a load of tripe.

The only person I've ever seen eating tripe is my nan. She used to boil it in milk. It was a yellowy white that looked and smelled absolutely disgusting. Is it the inside of a cow's stomach or something like that? I can guarantee you that I never touched it. Never in a million years would I ever want to eat that stuff.

And that's exactly how I feel about drugs too.

* * *

I've never fallen out with anyone I've got to know, and I think they'd say the same about me. I'm proud of that too. For me to dislike someone, they'd have to do something really bad.

When you get out of bed every day, if you spend two minutes thinking about what you can do for someone else, rather than all day thinking about what they can do for you, you'll be a good person and you'll be well liked. I don't know who said that first, but I wish it was me.

My mam was an exceptionally kind person, always helping others, but every so often she'd blow a fuse. And so do I. For me it's a culmination of turning a blind eye to the odd snidey remark in the pubs or nightclubs of South Shields or Jarrow, and people giving me a hard time there or at work. I can go a year or so without confrontation. Then on the odd occasion I'll let my guard down and let myself down. It's not the right thing to do, even in self-defence. It's something that I regret.

However, these setbacks will never stop me going above and beyond to help people: giving them a lift somewhere, presenting trophies, coaching kids and making people laugh.

When I was a teenager, not long after I passed my test, I was out driving and saw a woman next to her car, which had a flat tyre. So I stopped and fixed it for her, and then I was on my way without giving it another thought.

Ten years later a woman came up to me and said, 'Hullo. You don't remember me, do you?'

I said, 'No, sorry.'

'Can you remember changing a tyre for me about ten years ago?'

'You're joking. Was that you?'

'You know,' she said, 'I was standing there for 20 minutes while hundreds of cars passed by, but you were the only person who stopped to help. Thank you.'

It's little things like that – people remembering something kind you've done – that make you feel that you're a good person.

* * *

When I worked in sports development, what I enjoyed most was coaching young people with disabilities. In

30 years of working for the council, I coached young people with learning difficulties, Down's syndrome, Asperger's, dyspraxia, other physical difficulties, ADHD and behavioural problems.

Okay, I was paid a wage for that, but not always. One year there was a fun run in Middlesbrough (about an hour away from Jarrow), and I went down to help a girl with cerebral palsy. She could run a little bit before, but that day she ran six miles, which was a long distance for me but much further for her. We ran every step together. She must have felt great about herself to have run all that way.

And so did I. I'd been invited to run with her because of my athletics. But that day I wasn't thinking about my own running. I was giving something back.

* * *

Jimmy was always a great support to me. He could never do enough to help. He always said that I might have been a bit mad on motorbikes and this and that, but he knew I was a good lad. I still can't believe the amount of time he devoted to my athletics and the love he showed towards me. He had my interests at heart, not only as an athlete but as a whole person. What a positive impact he had on me. I learned a lot from Jimmy from the way he treated others with respect. It was the same with my mam, dad and nanna. The way they are towards you, they pass something on to you.

Growing up to become a good athlete and quite popular, what I also lacked – which I suppose might have made me a better athlete – was arrogance. I'd like to think that I'm still not arrogant. I'm not one to blow my own trumpet. I never introduce myself as an ex-athlete or bring athletics into a conversation unless the other person asks me first. If they're going to hear about me as an athlete at all, I'd rather they heard it from a third party than from me. I like to take people as I find them and for them to do the same with me.

The only people who've decided not to like me are some who haven't got to know me. One of the times that happened was on the weekend of the Great North Run. Every year, people always ask me if I'm running it or why I'm not running it. I have to explain that it's not my distance, even if I was still running. What those people don't realise is that I've been asked the same question only a few minutes earlier and I'll be asked it again a few minutes later. It's monotonous but it's good for learning patience.

One night, years after I retired from athletics, I was sitting in a pub called The Mechanics, which was full of people who had just finished the Great North Run. Next to me was a guy, half-cut, wearing his finishers' T-shirt and medal. He asked me, 'Did you do the run?'

Assuming that he'd recognised me, I said, 'No, it's too far for me. How did you get on though?'

'I did okay but it was my first run and I should do more training if I want to do better next year.'

'Have you thought about joining a club? There's one just down the road: South Shields Harriers. And there's one just up the road: Jarrow & Hebburn Athletics Club.'

'Oh, Jarrow. Aye, Jarra. Steve Cram.'

At this stage I still thought he knew who I was. But he didn't have a clue. Neither did I.

'Aye,' he continued. 'Steve Cram, the Jarrow Arrow. I used to really like him but I couldn't stand his mate. What was he called?'

Still not realising that he hadn't recognised me, I thought he was talking about somebody else.

'The one that was always clarting about and getting into trouble with the police,' he went on. 'I canna remember his name though. Ginger-haired nut.'

So I looked at him: a drunk bloke with his medal and T-shirt. And he looked at me: a bloke with no hair. Finally, the penny dropped for me. I went, 'David Sharpe?'

'David Sharpe, that's him. Used to call himself Sharpey. A right arsehole.'

By this time I was wondering how I was going to deal with this, so I asked him, 'What is it you don't like about him?'

'Ah, I've never liked him. I used to see him running on the telly but he was always in trouble. You're always hearing stories about him. Canna be bothered with him.'

After an awkward pause, I asked, 'What do you think about me?'

'You? I think you're a canny lad, aye.'

'So, if you like someone, he's a canny lad. But if you don't like someone, he's an arsehole?' I said, and then I asked him, 'Can I ask you something?'

'Aye.'

'Do you know what my name is?'

'Naw.'

'David Sharpe.'

'Oh.'

'You just said I'm a canny lad, but before that you said I was an arsehole. I cannot be both, can I?'

Do you know what he said to that?

'What happened to your hair?'

Well, I was a bit upset about what he'd said, but we didn't get into a fight or anything. We just picked up our pints and walked away in opposite directions.

He'd based his impression of me on what he'd heard from other people. But when he started to get to know me, even though he didn't know it was me, he thought differently.

The moral of the story is that we should take people as we find them and make up our own minds, rather than making assumptions based on gossip. But I suppose you could say that I asked for that. For all that I ran fast times, won big races, was on the telly and this and that, and for all that I like to help people, make them laugh and get along with everyone, I'm still nuts sometimes.

Although I've learned a lot and calmed down, I don't suppose I'll ever stop being that wild child from Jarrow.

Epilogue
Eagle Fever

The Highlands, Scotland, the 2000s

AS A child, I was always interested in the birds in the back garden. My fascination with birds of prey didn't really get started until I was 18 or 19. I read about Mike Tomkies, who was from the North East and used to run 800 metres. He became a famous Hollywood journalist and filmmaker who was well known by stars like Cary Grant, Omar Sharif and Dean Martin. He was known as 'The Wilderness Man', with his accounts of grizzly bears, cougars, bald eagles and killer whales in remote parts of Canada and all over the world. Eventually he settled down in a shack on the shore of Loch Shiel in the Scottish Highlands, where he filmed and wrote about wildcats, pine martens … and golden eagles.

Mike Tomkies inspired me. There were parts of his life that I related to. Not all of it, of course, but obviously I'm also from the North East, and I was running in different parts of the world. I didn't have time to spend days on end in the Highlands, but if I could have swapped my lifestyle for his when he was living in his lochside shack that could be reached only by boat, I'd have done it at the drop of a hat.

I really wanted to go in search of golden eagles and their eyries. Typically, it wasn't enough for me to watch them through binoculars from hundreds of metres away. I needed to get nearer. Not to touch them, like when I trapped blackbirds in my garden, but to be right up close.

You've heard of summit fever, when mountaineers get affected by altitude. Well, when I retired from athletics in the mid-90s, I had more time to catch *eagle fever*. I'd stop at nothing to reach an eyrie, regardless of the risks or dangers.

My first sight of a golden eagle was on the Isle of Arran, in the Firth of Clyde. Arran, although it's in the lower half of Scotland and only an hour's ferry ride away from a busy part of the mainland, is remote. It's described as a miniature Scotland, divided by the Highland Line. In the south, rolling farmland. To the north, rugged mountains. And golden eagles.

Looking for a golden eagle can be like trying to find a needle in a haystack. But I'd heard about this pair on Arran. The eyrie had been there for more than 20 years, lived in by different pairs. From a campsite way down in the glen you can just about see the eyrie on a sheer cliff face. It took hours to hike to it, and when you got there you weren't allowed anywhere near it.

But me being me, with my eagle fever, it was do or die to get to the top and get as close to them as I could get away with. The campsite was put on the back burner as I climbed higher and higher, in my shorts, long-sleeved running top and walking boots, fighting off vicious midges. Hours later I looked back down at the campsite with tents like dots, even through binoculars. I knew there wasn't much light left, and it felt like I had too far left to climb. Maybe I should have turned back.

Then, soaring high above in the distance, was a pair of golden eagles. It inspired me to keep going, even though there was no real path now, and it was nearly vertical. Eagle fever was driving me onwards and upwards, into the mist, up and up to the top of the crag where I'd seen the eagles flying.

When I eventually struggled to the summit, it was a big let-down because the eagles had disappeared. And there was no eyrie. So there I was, sitting on the cold, damp crag. Up on one of the highest points of the island, but down in the dumps. Was I on the wrong crag?

Some golden eagle eyries are four or five feet wide and the same deep. Not twigs, but branches. They shouldn't be that difficult to spot but I couldn't see it, and I was fed up, thinking about setting off, all the way back down the mountain, having wasted all that time.

I'll never forget what happened next. No more than 20 metres away, a golden eagle, eight-foot wingspan, flew close over my head. It was unbelievable, awe-inspiring. What was even better was that it had a rabbit in its talons, and within a couple of seconds of me seeing it, I heard *eeyock, eeyock, eeyock*. That's the noise a chick makes when it sees its parents coming with food.

At that moment the mist lifted and I looked across a crevasse to an almost identical crag on the other side, where there was an almost full-grown eagle chick jumping up and down, wings fully stretched, ready to fly the eyrie, and going *yok, yok-yok*. I was looking at a sheer drop, and it was getting late, but I just had to clamber my way around to get closer to the eyrie. It was like a dream come true, and I wasn't going to miss what could be one chance in a lifetime.

When I got there I couldn't believe it. After all that hiking and climbing, it was what birders would class as a walk-in. Normally, when the RSPB are ringing chicks, they have to be lowered down on a rope, but this one was easy. I didn't actually walk into the eyrie obviously, but I watched that chick from only a few metres away. White head, breast and legs; black and white feathers fluffed up; hooked, yellow beak and strong talons with black tips, busy tearing this rabbit apart; intelligent, black eyes. Beautiful.

It was one of the best experiences of my life. Years of anticipation and preparation, all the work I put in to reach my peak, achieving a lifetime ambition. It was like winning a major athletics championship.

Most things about golden eagles are kept secret, Arran included. The next day I was in a craft shop when the assistant asked me what I was doing on the island. I was that excited that I couldn't help myself. I described my experience, how I'd got a bit too close to the eyrie, that I didn't want to upset anyone, but it was all okay.

And she said, 'Can you do me a favour? If I give you the number, could you ring this guy? He looks after all the golden eagles on Arran and monitors the eyries. The one you've found is really remote, and I think he'd like to hear from you.'

'Okay, I will do,' I said. 'I know I'm not meant to be doing what I'm doing. But I'm not doing any harm, I didn't disturb them and I was only watching for ten minutes.'

'That's okay,' she said. 'He'd really like to hear about it.'

I wasn't sure whether I wanted to ring him or not. But the eyrie being so remote, it could have been a pair of golden eagles that he wasn't sure about, so maybe I'd be helping him, even though I shouldn't really have been there. It took me a few days to phone him, and I was back home. I said that the shop assistant had asked me to ring, that I'd been out walking and came across a golden eagle's eyrie. I was telling it like it was an accident, which wasn't true because I was up there looking for the eyrie. But I wasn't going to tell him that.

'What?' he said. 'What's your name? What were you doing up there?'

'I was out walking.'

'And you just happened to bump into this golden eagle eyrie, did you? Do you not mean you were looking for it?'

'Well, I was birdwatching.'

'Do you not know it's illegal to be up there? Those eagles have been there for years, and no one's ever been that close to them before. Up here we like to leave them in peace. But we've got people like you coming up and ...'

He went on and on, and I was getting annoyed with him.

'You know what it is, mate?' I interrupted him. 'Take a hike. I've just been doing this as a favour. I was asked to ring you. You know, it doesn't matter.' And I put the phone down on him.

It had been a trap, and I'd walked straight into it. The shop assistant had set me up, and I'd fallen for it. At least it wasn't as dangerous as when I was taken in by the hotel receptionist sending me to that pub in Belfast.

The law with eagles is a bit of a grey area. You cannot disturb an eyrie of a breeding pair during the breeding months, about May to July. That's when you might interfere with the nesting, and if they fail, you'll get the blame. And that's fair enough.

But I could pay someone £30 to go on a wildlife tour in a minibus full of people provided with binoculars and a telescope. And that's okay, you can see the eyries without having what's called a Schedule 1 licence for observing protected species. I was finding eyries off my own back, and I haven't got a licence, but neither have these people on the minibus tour. There shouldn't be one rule for one and another rule for another.

Anyway, I'd got into trouble for getting too close. People on bird forums were saying, 'Who do you think you are? You need a licence.' It was one thing after another, a pain in the backside because of the legality of things. Sometimes birdwatching was like a chore and I wondered if it was worth all the bother.

That wasn't the only time I got into trouble. Me being me, I had to keep looking for eagles.

A few years ago I got a book of maps with six-figure grid references, which cost £60 and should never have been published. There was a hell of a fuss about it, because there were sites of eyries on the maps. I got wind of a sea eagle eyrie in a remote part of the Highlands. Silke was with me, and she said, 'You do know it's the breeding season, don't you?'

But I said it would be aareet. Well, I would say that, wouldn't I?

We were driving up a track where we shouldn't have been, when the landowner pulled up in his posh Land Rover. 'Excuse me,' he said. 'You can't go up there. It's trespassing.'

'Okay,' I said, 'but actually I'm interested in sea eagles.'

'Well, there aren't any up there.' And I was thinking, *Well, I know there are some up there.*

The landowner started to drive off, then he stopped at a bend and looked back at me and at the river where we'd parked our car. So the farmer was looking at me by the river, and I was looking at him on the bend, and I said to Silke, 'I don't know what this guy's problem is, he keeps looking round the bend at me and the river.'

All of a sudden, Silke said, 'Look what's in the river.'

We hadn't had much rain that summer, so the water level was really low. And there, on the riverbed, were these huge black things like stones. Freshwater mussels. They can live to 150 years on the bottom of riverbeds. They're in only a handful of Scottish rivers, usually difficult to find. But we could see hundreds of them. It was a rare sight, and I wasn't even looking for them.

Some freshwater mussels have pearls inside, and there's a black market for them. People get them out of the water and crack them open, which of course is illegal. Now I knew why the landowner was looking at me so suspiciously.

But I was only interested in the sea eagles. Ironically, disturbing eagles up on high or freshwater mussels down below can lead to similar consequences if you're caught disturbing either of them. And here I was, too close for comfort to both species. I wasn't having a good day at all, and Silke was becoming agitated.

'We need to go,' she said. 'I told you that we shouldn't be up here anyway.'

'But I want to see the eyrie. I'll just have a quick look at it from down below. I won't be long,' I promised Silke. It was just like when I was a kid: I had to get my own way.

So off I went with our dog, and eventually we ended up out in the middle of nowhere, with Silke waiting back in the car, bored stiff. I hadn't seen a dickie bird for a couple of hours, when all of a sudden a huge sea eagle – magnificent, soaring on the thermals, totally relaxed, smooth, majestic – flew over me and landed on its eyrie, which I hadn't even noticed. I was like, *I don't believe this is happening.*

I was so busy watching the sea eagle that I hadn't noticed the dog was getting a bit distressed. And then I heard this *moooo-oooo.* We were surrounded by cows that had crept up on us through the ferns. I knew they were after the dog, not me. I also knew that people can get trampled to death by cows. I started panicking because we were in a dangerous situation. Instead of going round the winding way we'd come, I decided to take the direct route through the rough fern and spiky heather, down the steep slope to Silke and the car. I was shiteing myself, but I took a run for it, camera and binoculars bouncing all over, dog panting alongside, cows chasing us.

Eventually we made it back to the car, when who should come round the bend? The landowner. Who went ballistic. 'I'm sick of you lot coming up here! Can you lot leave these birds alone? You know it's against the law.'

I let him say his piece. He did have a point, so I said, 'I apologise, but all I wanted was one photograph.'

'That's one photograph too many!'

I'd driven up a track where we weren't allowed, saw hundreds of freshwater mussels that didn't even interest me, spotted a sea eagle, nearly reached the eyrie, didn't take any photographs, got chased by a herd of cows, and now I was getting told off by the landowner. Well, I started to get a bit peed off with the way he was going on and on, but I kept quiet, got in the car and we drove away.

We'd only driven about half a mile when Silke said, 'Pull over.'

'What's the matter, like?' I asked.

'I'm going to vomit.'

After she'd thrown up, she said, 'I never wanted to come out with you anyway. You just can't leave things alone, can you? You've always got to get your own way. You said you wouldn't be long, but you were ages. And now you're in trouble again. I told you this would happen, but you wouldn't listen. Instead of just watching from a distance like everybody else, you have to go and upset people. Right, that's it! The next time you go looking for eagles, you're on your own. I've had enough! I'm sick of you!'

The thing is, once I get my head into something, I get intrigued and I've got to see it through to the end. So, a normal, relaxing holiday ended up being a major scene. And all I'd wanted to do was to see the eagles.

I've been doing this for 30 years, but I still haven't done what I really want to do. Because although I've got one photograph of one eagle chick on one eyrie,

I wish I could film an adult eagle in its eyrie with its chick.

Once I've done that I might be able to finally relax a little bit. It's my golden ambition.

Competition Record

David Sharpe
Date of birth: 8 July 1967
Club: Jarrow & Hebburn AC

Major International Honours
World Junior Champion, 800m, 1986
European Indoor Champion, 800m, 1988
Silver, European Championships, 800m, 1990
World Cup Winner, 800m, 1992

Personal Bests
800m: 1:43.98, 1992
800m indoor: 1:46.92, 1993
1000m: 2:17.79, 1992
1000m indoor: 2:20.36, 1986
1500m: 3:42.7, 1985 (3:42.77, 1986)
1500m indoor: 3:46.21, 1986
One Mile: 3:59.01, 1990

Selected competitions
Key
Bold = season's best time
(i) = indoors
h = heat
sf = semi-final

Date	Competition	Venue	Distance	Pos.	Time
1984 *(age 16/17)*					
4 July	Tyne League	Gateshead	1500m	2	**3:46.3**
17 July	Highland Games	Edinburgh	1000m	3	**2:24.06**
N/K	Invitational	Byrkjelo, Norway	800m	N/K	**1:51.02**
1985 *(age 17/18)*					
N/K	UK Championships	Antrim	800m	2	**1:49.32**
25 August	European Junior Championships	Cottbus, Germany	800m	8	1:53.38
17 October	Tyne League	Gateshead	1500m	1	**3:42.7**
1986 *(age 18/19)*					
25 January	AAA Indoor Championships	Cosford	800m	1	1:49.48 (i)
8 February	England v Hungary	Cosford	800m	1	**1:48.53 (i)**
22 February	European Indoor Championships	Madrid, Spain	800m	4 (h)	1:53.93 (i)
25 February	England v Soviet Union	Cosford	1500m	3	**3:46.21 (i)**
8 March	England v USA	Cosford	1000m	1	**2:20.36 (i)**

19 April	Road race	South Shields	10K	2	**30:19**
3 May	Invitation	Gateshead	One Mile	1	**4:01.0**
26 May	UK Championships	Cwmbran	800m	2	1:47.01
15 June	Invitation	Ipswich	800m	2	1:46.8
17 June	England v USA	Gateshead	800m	1	1:45.88
21 June	AAA Championships	Crystal Palace, London	800m	3	1:46.81
5 July	Bislett Games	Oslo, Norway	1500m	11	**3:42.77**
18 July	World Junior Championships	Athens, Greece	800m	1	1:48.32
20 July	World Junior Championships	Athens, Greece	1500m	5	3:46.94
5 August	England v Commonwealth	Gateshead	1000m	1	2:19.41
11 August	Grand Prix	Brussels, Belgium	1000m	7	2:19.58
19 August	Dairy Crest	Birmingham	1000m	6	**2:18.98**
5 September	Ivo Van Damme Memorial	Brussels, Belgium	800m	5	**1:45.64**
12 September	Mcvitie's Challenge	Crystal Palace, London	800m	2	1:46.40

1987
(age 19/20)

5 February	Invitational	Melbourne, Australia	1500m	3	**3:44.5**
17 June	Invitational	Gateshead	800m	2	1:47.0
4 July	Bislett Games	Oslo, Norway	800m	2	**1:46.09**
13 July	Invitational	Nice, France	800m	7	1:47.10
26 July	Pearl Assurance	Gateshead	800m	3	1:48.39
14 August	Invitational	London	800m	5	1:46.89
22 August	Invitational	London	800m	3	1:47.61

1988
(age 20/21)

20 February	Invitational	Athens, Greece	800m	1	**1:47.32 (i)**
6 March	European Indoor Championships	Budapest, Hungary	800m	1	1:49.17 (i)
12 March	Invitational	Cosford	800m	1	1:48.36 (i)
1 June	Invitational	Sevilla, Spain	800m	5	1:46.30
11 June	Invitational	Casablanca, Morocco	800m	1	1:46.91
15 June	Invitational	Gateshead	800m	2	1:47.6
2 July	Bislett Games	Oslo, Norway	800m	5	**1:45.70**
8 July	Peugeot Games	London	800m	7	1:47.36
10 July	Invitational	Nice, France	800m	7	1:46.74
29 July	Invitational	Edinburgh	1000m	2	**2:19.89**
6 August	AAA Championships	Birmingham	800m	4	1:45.98
14 August	Invitational	Gateshead	800m	1	1:48.66
28 August	Invitational	London	800m	4	1:47.95
31 August	Invitational	Rieti, Italy	1000m	6	2:28.58

1989
(age 21/22)

19 February	European Indoor Championships	The Hague, Netherlands	800m	DNF	n/a (**1:51.06** sf)
24 June	GB v West Germany, Soviet Union & USA	Birmingham	800m	5	1:47.51
7 July	Invitational	Edinburgh	800m	8	**1:47.20**

1990
(age 22/23)

23 February	GB v East Germany	Glasgow	1000m	1	**2:23.50 (i)**
27 May	Invitational	Battersea Park, London	One Mile	7	**3:59.02**
20 June	Invitational	Bratislava, Czechoslovakia	800m	4	1:46.02
29 June	Dairy Crest	Gateshead	800m	3	1:47.71
6 July	Grand Prix	Edinburgh	800m	3	1:45.86
14 July	Bislett Games	Oslo, Norway	800m	3	**1:45.12**
16 July	Invitational	Belfast	800m	1	1:46.93
20 July	Parcelforce	Crystal Palace, London	800m	5	1:45.42
4 August	AAA Championships	Birmingham	800m	4	1:45.80
13 August	Invitational	Grosseto, Italy	800m	1	1:46.30
17 August	Pearl Assurance	Gateshead	800m	3	1:46.69
29 August	European Championships	Split, Yugoslavia	800m	2	1:45.59
16 September	Mcvitie's Challenge	Sheffield	800m	4	1:46.98

1991
(age 23/24)

26 January	Pas de Calais	Lievin, France	800m	3	**1:51.10**
2 June	Invitational	Chania, Crete	800m	1	**1:46.63**
19 June	GB v Germany	Crystal Palace, London	800m	4	1:47.51
1 July	Invitational	Lille, France	1000m	1	**2:19.50**

3 July	Invitational	Stockholm, Sweden	800m	10	1:54.60
12 July	Parcelforce	Crystal Palace, London	800m	7	1:47.90
27 July	AAA Championships	Birmingham	800m	6	1:47.54
9 August	Pearl Assurance	Gateshead	800m	4	1:46.86

1992
(age 24/25)

17 June	Invitational	Verona, Italy	800m	2	1:45.95
28 June	AAA Championships	Birmingham	800m	4	1:45.61
10 July	TSB	Crystal Palace, London	800m	3	1:45.25
17 July	Vauxhall	Gateshead	800m	1	1:45.09
14 August	Lucozade	Sheffield	800m	1	1:46.06
19 August	Weltklasse	Zürich, Switzerland	800m	1	**1:43.98**
28 August	Invitational	Brussels, Belgium	800m	1	1:45.32
31 August	Les Jones Memorial	Belfast	1000m	1	**2:17.79**
4 September	Invitational	Turin, Italy	800m	8	1:47.05
6 September	Invitational	Rieti, Italy	800m	4	1:44.67
25 September	World Cup	Havana, Cuba	800m	1	1:46.06

1993
(age 25/26)

30 January	GB v Russia	Glasgow	800m	2	**1:46.92 (i)**
13 February	GB v USA	Birmingham	800m	1	1:47.76 (i)

5 June	Pearl Assurance European Relays	Portsmouth	4x800m	3	(7:12.66)
13 June	UK Championships	Crystal Palace, London	800m	2	1:47.12
10 July	Bislett Games	Oslo, Norway	800m	4	1:47.32
23 July	TSB	Crystal Palace, London	800m	7	1:49.19
30 July	Vauxhall	Gateshead	800m	4	**1:46.09**

1995
(age 27/28)

2 May	Invitational	Forte-de-France	800m	4	**1:51.00**
2 July	BUPA Games	Gateshead	800m	DNF	n/a